AN ARMY OF
PROBLEM SOLVERS

ALSO BY SHAUN LONEY

BUILD Prosperity: Energizing Manitoba's Local Economy

Available for free download at: http://buildinc.ca/ build-prosperity/

AN ARMY OF
PROBLEM SOLVERS

RECONCILIATION AND THE SOLUTIONS ECONOMY

BY SHAUN LONEY
WITH WILL BRAUN

Library and Archives Canada Cataloguing in Publication

Loney, Shaun, author
An army of problem solvers / by Shaun Loney with Will Braun.

Includes bibliographical references and index.
ISBN 978-0-9952685-0-0 (paperback)

1. Social responsibility of business. 2. Social entrepreneurship.
3. Sustainable development. 4. Community development.
5. Economic development. I. Braun, Will, 1973-, author II. Title.

HD60.L63 2016   658.4'08   C2016-905591-4

Printed in Canada by Friesens
Cover design & interior design by Jess Koroscil

WHAT'S BEING SAID ABOUT
AN ARMY OF PROBLEM SOLVERS:

*"Ground-breaking Canadian social entrepreneur Shaun
Loney shows how it's done. Innovation that leaves you asking,
'Why isn't everyone doing this already?'"*
—MICHAEL TOYE, EXECUTIVE DIRECTOR OF THE CANADIAN
COMMUNITY ECONOMIC DEVELOPMENT NETWORK

*"Shaun Loney connects the dots and articulates a way forward.
This book is for everyone who cares about reconciliation."*
—MOLLY MCCRACKEN, DIRECTOR OF THE CANADIAN
CENTRE FOR POLICY ALTERNATIVES MANITOBA OFFICE

*"I've long written about a new green economy that was possible.
Now, Shaun Loney is making it happen. Bravo to the whole team!!!"*
—WAYNE ROBERTS, AUTHOR OF NO-NONSENSE GUIDE
TO WORLD FOOD AND FOOD FOR CITY BUILDING

*"Shaun Loney's ideas are simultaneously simple and ingenious.
Start a revolution; read this book!"*
—DR. EVELYN FORGET, PROFESSOR OF ECONOMICS AND
CANADA'S LEADING EXPERT ON GUARANTEED ANNUAL INCOME

*"This book is a timely and important milestone in the
journey towards rebuilding a social value marketplace."*
—DAVID LEPAGE, FOUNDER AND CEO OF BUY SOCIAL
AND FOUNDER OF ENTERPRISING NON-PROFITS

*"To solve our most stubborn problems we need more
innovative thinking – and this book points the way."*
—PAUL VOGT, PRESIDENT OF RED RIVER COLLEGE AND FORMER
CABINET SECRETARY TO MANITOBA'S GARY DOER GOVERNMENT

"Loney offers convincing evidence that social entrepreneurs have answers that business and government don't."
—JULIA DEANS, EXECUTIVE DIRECTOR OF FUTURPRENEUR

"On behalf of the team, we are so pleased to see this second book. We're glad to be on the front lines of the solutions revolution."
—LUCAS STEWART, CO-FOUNDER SOCIAL ENTERPRISE CENTRE AND MANITOBA GREEN RETROFIT

"Making it easy for problem solvers - now that's fresh thinking. Thanks Shaun Loney for this timely and inspiring work!"
—WADOOD IBRAHIM, CO-FOUNDER OF PROTEGRA AND CHAIR OF THE BOARD OF THE WINNIPEG CHAMBER OF COMMERCE (2016-2017)

"No better manual exists for how enterprise, community spirit, innovation and determination, really can and do make good things happen"
—HUGH SEGAL, MASTER, MASSEY COLLEGE

"A real-world exploration of the ups and downs of tackling some of Canada's most intractable problems. A must read for those trying to bring forward systemic change."
—JEFF CYR, FORMER EXECUTIVE DIRECTOR OF THE NATIONAL ASSOCIATION OF FRIENDSHIP CENTRES AND CHAIR OF THE INDIGENOUS ADVISORY BOARD OF THE CANADIAN INSTITUTES OF HEALTH RESEARCH

"Colonization put dysfunction into our families and our economies. Ideas like what Aki Energy offers are a path to decolonization which replaces the dysfunction with love and compassion."
—PAUL LACERTE, CO-FOUNDER MOOSEHIDE CAMPAIGN

"A fabulous collection of economic development stories from places where economic development is needed most."
—SENATOR ART EGGLETON

"Indigenous social innovation will rebuild vibrant Indigenous culture and economies in Canada. This book is an important contribution."
—NICOLE MCDONALD, MCCONNELL FOUNDATION

TABLE OF
CONTENTS

ACKNOWLEDGMENTS

I want to thank Will Braun. In many ways he's been a co-writer, challenging me when needed and being enthusiastic enough to remind me that this story is important. I was also encouraged to write by Paul Vogt who worked in the very highest levels of the Gary Doer Government. He's a pragmatic guy and it has been important to me to be reminded that the ideas in this book are not only necessary but practical.

My co-workers at the Social Enterprise Centre are simply amazing. Lucas Stewart (Che) has been on board since the beginning. Annetta Armstrong and Art Ladd do a great job of running BUILD. It's good to have colleagues at Aki Energy like Darcy Wood (mentor, teacher, and #1 Ogimaa), Kate Taylor (making all things possible), Ray Starr, and Rodney Contois. Our board at Aki Energy, including Sam Murdock and Jerry Woods, believes in us enough to say "Go for it!" Beyond Winnipeg, the broader circle of inspiration and ingenuity includes Kristin Nickel at Brandon Energy Efficiency Program in Brandon, Manitoba; Sheldon Pollett at Impact Construction in St. John's, Newfoundland; and Marc Soberano at Building Up in Toronto.

I also want to give my appreciation to Cree Elder, the Very Reverend Stan McKay and Grand Chief Sheila North Wilson for supporting the writing of this book. Reconciliation is as much about Aboriginal people as it is about non-Aboriginal people. I'm pleased to bring my voice to the national discussion of what reconciliation really means.

My partner, Fiona, is an incredible innovator – always a decade or so ahead of most everyone else. I learn a lot about feminism from hanging around her. At its core, the movement is about power – who has it, who doesn't, and what can bring more balance. I only had the courage to get involved in the social enterprise movement after we got together.

The three young men in my life are also my best friends. My sons Weslee and Owen, and Fiona's son Aandeg, are all finding their own way. Belonging to each other is an incredible gift. They daily remind me that the best approach to life is simply to "leave the campsite better than how we found it."

Love and gratitude also to my dad who taught me to like the world enough to love it and to my mom who taught me to love the world enough to change it.

Lastly, a note on the title. I have spent a fair bit of time with Gene Stolzfus who was the founding director of Christian Peacemaker Teams. He once told me that it was entirely possible to have prevented the US army from invading Iraq. All that was needed, he said, "was an army of peacemakers." So for any of you who find the title of this book a bit abrasive, know that it is inspired by one of the greatest peacemakers of our time.

—*Shaun Loney, July 1ˢᵗ, 2016*

PREFACE
BY GRAND CHIEF SHEILA NORTH WILSON

I am a proud member of the Bunibonibee Cree Nation. I was born and raised there, on the shore of Oxford Lake in northern Manitoba, surrounded by so many family members and friends. We spent lots of time trapping, fishing, snow machining, boating, and just being outside. But in the midst of all this beauty, there was something missing.

None of us had much hope for our economic future. There were very few jobs on the First Nation – and the jobs that were there were mostly filled by outsiders.

Lack of opportunity, lack of jobs, and lack of hope can only lead a people in one direction. Murdered and missing Indigenous women, deeply ingrained poverty, massive unemployment, rampant diabetes, and a critical shortage of housing and basic infrastructure touch each and every family in one way or another.

It never used to be this way. My grandparents told me that when they were young, everyone had a role to play. At the root of our healthy economies was hard work, shared prosperity, and respect for our communities and for Mother Earth. My people got their own food – we hunted, we fished, we gathered, and we gardened. We looked after our own energy needs too by cutting wood. We did all this in a way that respected our communities and, of course, Mother Earth. I don't say this to make it sound romantic. There was plenty of hardship. But we thrived.

Canadians are just now beginning to hear about what actually happened. Introduced into our story were unfulfilled treaties, reserves, loss of land, residential schools, and the sixties scoop – governments have recognized these wrongs, apologized, supported the Truth and Reconciliation Commission, and endorsed its Calls to Action, but now what?

An Army of Problem Solvers: Reconciliation and the Solutions Economy has come around at the right time for the right reasons. Shaun

Loney's work is informed and inspired by the people he works with. As he says, reflecting upon a journey of Indigenous and non-Indigenous people towards a common goal of mutual well-being, this is "our story." What we want for ourselves, we also want for each other. After all, isn't that what the treaties are all about?

It's possible - I don't know for sure - that most Canadians think that it is up to us First Nations people to figure this out. But we can't do this alone. We'll do our part for sure. Our people are ready. But right now the rules are stacked against us.

Most Canadians know that our education system is underfunded, for example, but do they know that, in the midst of unemployment and diabetes crises, there is no meaningful support for local food production – and that our food has to compete against federally subsidized monopoly retailers whose businesses are making us sick? Do they know that, in the middle of the urgency of climate change, the federal government bureaucracy actively suppresses the expansion of First Nation geothermal social enterprises? Do Canadians know that, in the midst of all this talk about self-government, at least in Manitoba, it is illegal for First Nations people to generate our own power and sell it even to ourselves?

Well, thanks to *An Army of Problem Solvers*, they know now. As Shaun explains, while governments were busy trying to "take the Indian out of the child," they were also "taking the Indian out of the economy" and what's more problematic in this present period of reconciliation is that it's still actively happening.

In the midst of all this, our people are beginning to assert our own economic rights. Relying heavily on work already being done in our communities by Aki Energy and others, I recently compiled and released a 10-point community-based economic action plan that focuses on the federal and provincial governments acting in such a way "so as to allow the re-emergence of local economies," as Shaun says.

At the heart of this strategy is a big step towards creating a new Nation-to-Nation relationship. Shaun's book defines more clearly what this means. Nation-to-Nation doesn't just mean getting rid of diesel fuel in remote communities, it means having our own utilities that sell renewable energy to heat and power our homes. Nation-to-Nation doesn't mean simply making imported food more affordable, it means transforming our local food economies. Nation-to-Nation doesn't mean raising social assistance rates, it means implementing a basic income guarantee. Nation-to-Nation even includes having our own currencies (alongside Canadian currency) that promote local businesses.

The Elders are telling me that they recognize the value in the economies that we are trying to build. Much of what we are proposing is focused around community-led economic activity. Many people are calling these ventures social enterprises. The values are old but still so relevant today, and they will form the core of how we move forward.

I remember the year because I was 20 and pregnant with my first child. Word got out that there was going to be someone coming into our community to offer driver licensing. We all knew that a driver's license was a ticket to freedom, so practically the entire community signed up! Having a license meant we could apply for jobs both on and off the reserve. There was a real sense of optimism that, all too commonly, was dashed when the service was only offered for a couple of days.

Shaun correctly says that prosperity is the antidote to poverty. We are indeed entering into a new era. We are going to focus more on problem solving and less on the problems. After reading this book, I'm even more optimistic. Let's do it.

— *Grand Chief Sheila North Wilson*
Manitoba Keewatinowi Okimakanak (MKO)

AN ARMY OF
PROBLEM SOLVERS

LAYING THE
GROUNDWORK

CHAPTER 1

THE UPSIDE OF DOWN
CONFESSIONS OF AN EX-BUREAUCRAT

It was a sight that would not make any Canadian proud.

I stood outside a small bingo hall and watched as 85 percent of the adults in Garden Hill First Nation queued up in alphabetized lines to receive their welfare cheques. This is the bimonthly ritual on most First Nations, including Garden Hill, a fly-in community of about 4,000 people in northeastern Manitoba. While I was just visiting that day and would soon return to my home in Winnipeg, I realized that this is the reality for far too many Canadians, especially Indigenous people.

I followed the crowds from the bingo hall to several rickety docks. Typically, Garden Hill welfare recipients go straight down to the water's edge where they pay $5 per person to take a water taxi to the Northern Store on a nearby off-reserve island. The Northern Store is run by the Winnipeg-based North West Company, which dates back to the 1670s fur trade. The company runs over 120 stores across the North, where there is a definitive lack of competition.

These stores, including Garden Hill's, charge a fee to cash welfare cheques. This is the first point of economic leakage where the precious little money in the community quickly exits the local economy.

Then the Garden Hill welfare recipients buy groceries – many of them unhealthy, all of them expensive, and almost all of them shipped in by air. The store employs some locals, but nearly all revenues go south to large food suppliers, shippers, and North West Company shareholders.

Garden Hill is located on Island Lake, which offers one of the most beautiful views I've ever seen. But this beautiful place is also a place of deeply ingrained poverty, rampant diabetes, chronic unemployment, family breakdown, and high crime and incarceration rates. These ills tear the community apart and cost all levels of government a great deal of money.

As I stood and watched the money flow out of the community, I couldn't help but think how utterly naïve and ineffective society's usual responses are. Is the problem here that welfare rates are too low? Is the problem that people simply don't pull themselves up by their bootstraps? If you stand on the dock at Garden Hill, as I did on that cool spring day last May, watching people return from the Northern Store island, you either see a system desperately broken, or you see a series of opportunities.

In my early years as political staff and then senior civil servant in the NDP Government of Manitoba, I would have seen mostly problems – expensive problems. But my view has changed through more than a decade of on-the-ground experience in the field of social enterprise. I see things differently now, whether on a First Nation or in the broader society, whether in relation to diabetes, unemployment, incarceration, child welfare, or climate change. What I've learned has made me far more optimistic about the world.

THE SOLUTIONS ECONOMY

What I saw on the dock at Garden Hill was not poverty and dependence but opportunity. Instead of unemployment, I saw a ready workforce. Instead of a diabetes epidemic, I saw people who would buy healthy food if it were affordable and convenient. Instead of a high-priced monopoly retailer, I saw room for more market entrants. Instead of poorly spent government money, I saw ample opportunity for smarter investment. I think of it as the "upside of down," to borrow a term from Thomas Homer-Dixon.

My change in perspective has not come about from reading books or sitting in classrooms; it has come from the trenches. This book is rooted firmly in my decade-plus experience in helping to start and mentor 11 social enterprises that are realizing the upside of down in tangible ways. Most of my examples are from Manitoba, where my work is focused, but the lessons learned apply beyond provincial and national borders, and indeed, the solutions economy is growing all over the world.

Social enterprises are smaller-scale community businesses that use market forces to solve stubborn social or environmental challenges. They combine business smarts, common sense, ingenuity, community rootedness, and basic human caring. A more complete definition follows in the next chapter, as does a definition of the solutions economy, of which social enterprises form a key part.

In the latter part of the book, I discuss a cost-neutral Basic Income Guarantee, a $15 minimum wage, complementary currencies, and a transformative new model for child welfare. These measures would give people and their families the tools and resources that they need to be successful. The solutions economy takes a broad view, looking at how policies and practices interconnect across sectors and government departments. It is within this broader view that I have come to see a new role for government as essential to solving societal challenges.

RECONCILIATION

It has been important for me, on my own personal journey, to realize how it is that we got to a place where a First Nation called Garden Hill has no gardens. The ancestors of the current residents of Garden Hill built strong local economies. Everyone had a place doing things they were good at and working in a manner that was good for both the social fabric of the community and the surrounding environment.

Our national conversation right now is around the horrific impacts of residential schools, as it should be, but alongside the Canadian government's efforts to "take the Indian out of the child" was a range of other policies to "take the Indian out of the economy." Too many of those policies still persist to this day. I believe that changing them is one important and very tangible way to work at reconciliation.

Every day in my work, I and my courageous and creative colleagues and I see the problem-solving model in action. The great news is that it works! Since far too much poverty in Canada is located in Indigenous communities (urban, rural, and northern), much of my work and this book focus on that reality. But of course the solutions economy works across various demographics and regions.

AN ARMY OF HEROES

My introduction to the solutions economy came through my work with several social enterprises. This book arises very directly from those experiences. I am currently at Aki Energy, which I co-founded, along with Darcy Wood, Kate Taylor and Sam Murdock, in 2013. Based in Winnipeg, Aki serves as something of a social enterprise incubator, offering various supports and services for First Nations wanting to start their own social enterprises. We help with ideas, training, and the various steps required for setting up and operating a social enterprise. In most cases, we do not own the businesses – we just support and facilitate them. Our chief executive officer is Darcy Wood, the former chief of the Garden Hill First Nation.

In our first three years, Aki and our partners have installed $6 million of energy efficient geothermal energy systems in 350 homes on four First Nations in Manitoba. Each venture is a non-profit social enterprise with local employees doing the actual work. Eight crews of trained workers have already installed 213 kilometres of piping loop for geothermal systems that will cut utility bills by $15 million over the next 20 years. Peguis First Nation and the Fisher River Cree Nation have their own geothermal installation operations – the two largest in western Canada. Not only is this work paid for out of the utility bill reductions, it also creates sustainable, local employment. We intend to install $100 million worth of geothermal energy in the next decade in Manitoba alone. We are also branching out beyond the energy sector with Aki Foods, as you will read about in Chapter 4.

Prior to Aki, in 2006, I was on the team that co-founded BUILD (Building Urban Industries for Local Employment), a Winnipeg social enterprise that trains mostly people who have been in prison to do energy-saving and water-saving retrofits where low-income families live. I tell the story of BUILD in Chapter 7. It was my introduction into the world of social enterprise, and I am very proud to say that we were awarded ScotiaBank's EcoLiving Green Business of the Year in 2011, Manitoba Apprenticeship's Employer of the Year in 2013, and recipient of the Winnipeg Chamber of Commerce's Spirit Award in 2016.

SOCIAL ENTERPRISE CENTRE

BUILD

MGR
Manitoba Green Retrofit

Pollock's
HARDWARE CO-OP
CONTRACTOR STORE

THE SOCIAL ENTERPRISE CENTRE, LOCATED AT 765 MAIN STREET IN WINNIPEG'S NORTH END.

BUILD's model has been adopted in Brandon, Manitoba (Brandon Energy Efficiency Program, started in 2008), St. John's, Newfoundland (Impact Construction, 2010) and in Toronto (Building Up!, 2014).

I also want to tell you about Manitoba Green Retrofit (MGR, 2009), a social enterprise that hires BUILD's graduates to renovate apartments, install high-efficiency natural gas furnaces in low-income housing, and undertake bedbug remediation. Who would have thought there would be an upside to bedbugs?

Aki, BUILD, MGR, and others are housed at the Social Enterprise Centre, which we established in Winnipeg's North End in 2011. This 30,000 square foot building is itself a social enterprise. Not unlike a business park, the Social Enterprise Centre is an active hub that is incubating new social enterprises in Manitoba and beyond.

In each case, these ventures transform the economy, turning problems into opportunities and going where the government and private sector cannot or will not. The above examples are just a small sampling of what happens in the solutions economy – a sector that is broad, diverse, and becoming more and more so all the time.

There are pockets of the solutions economy emerging all over Canada – in inner city neighbourhoods and on First Nations. The same can be said outside of Canada as well. At Aki Energy in Winnipeg, we continue to be inspired by groups like Honor the Earth in Minnesota. Led by Indigenous activist, economist and writer Winona LaDuke, Honor the Earth put out a strategy on creating a "green economy for brown people" back in 2008. Aki has based its strategy and communications on this work.

Finally, I want to mention Ashoka, an international movement of social entrepreneurs. The organization supports more than 3,000 fellows who do an incredibly broad range of work in 84 countries. I am privileged to be one of those fellows, and it is partly through the support of Ashoka that I am able to offer you this book.

Ashoka is a wellspring of creativity within the solutions economy. Ashoka says that "problem solving is the skill around which the world is becoming increasingly organized." That is what the solutions economy is all about, and that is why I am so excited to be part of it. Each

MANITOBA GREEN RETROFIT STAFF SHIRT. WORK UNIFORMS ARE WORN PROUDLY, OFTEN REPLACING GANG COLOURS.

social enterprise is full of heroes, some of whom you'll meet in the following pages. While the dictionary defines a hero as "one who displays courage and self-sacrifice for the greater good," I've come to define heroes as "people who overcome incredible barriers to do the daily things that the rest of us have taken for granted."

This book is dedicated to the heroes with whom I've had the pleasure to journey and the ones whom I have yet to meet.

CHAPTER 2

WHO ARE THE PROBLEM SOLVERS?

HOW THE SOLUTIONS ECONOMY WORKS

The term "solutions economy," or "solutions sector" as it is sometimes called, is somewhat general and flexible. Different people define it in different ways. My own definition will come most clearly through the numerous concrete examples I provide in this book, but I'll offer a more concise definition here as well. The solutions economy is essentially about solving social and environmental problems by using market forces.

Within the solutions economy, challenges like climate change, high incarceration and re-incarceration rates, persistent poverty, and ballooning healthcare costs are addressed not by demanding more government spending, offering charity, or expecting free enterprise to solve all ills. It seeks out transformative, common-sense, real-world solutions from outside the box – or, as the Elders tell me, "from inside the circle."

The solutions economy criss-crosses the ideological spectrum, at times confounding both sides, more often winning them both over. It seeks collaboration, not polarization of sides. It is not an ideology, which is to say it is not about arguing that one economic school of thought is superior or that one political philosophy is the answer. It is not about being right in some abstract, theoretical way. It is about innovative, on-the-ground solutions.

You cannot solve a problem without a problem solver. In this book, I will explore the three main problem solvers:

- social enterprises;
- social entrepreneurs; and
- the small farm movement.

These categories are not exhaustive, nor is the terminology watertight. Terminology in this field is relatively new and is still evolving.

Different people use these terms in different ways. I'll try to be as clear as I can be in how I use them, while also leaving space for the natural blurring and blending that happens.

SOCIAL ENTERPRISE: THE BUSINESS OF CHANGE

Social enterprises are non-profit businesses that derive most of their income in the marketplace selling goods and services that improve social and/or environmental problems. They are usually small-scale economic entities that go where the private sector and governments cannot. They are very adept at affordably solving stubborn social and environmental problems.

A social enterprise could be a community-run market garden operation that outcompetes an outside-owned monopoly grocer on a remote First Nation (and reduces social assistance, health, and other service costs in the process). Or it could be a non-profit retrofit venture that hires people who are at a high risk of reoffending to improve energy efficiency in public housing, thus reducing energy bills and saving governments some of the exorbitant costs of re-incarcerating people (since employment turns out to be a really good way to keep people from returning to jail). Or it could be a church-run non-profit that employs formerly homeless people to make jams and preserves from B-grade fruit that would otherwise be discarded.

Again, these are not charities or government programs. They are economic entities using market forces. They combine the entrepreneurial savvy of the business sector with the community ethos of the non-profit sector. They are businesses of the people, by the people, and for the people.

SOCIAL ENTREPRENEURS: MAKING MONEY, MAKING CHANGE

A social entrepreneur is a business person who uses a typical business model but sells something that addresses a social or environmental problem. This could be a billionaire electric-vehicle manufacturer or a factory worker who salvages used steel pails from work, crushes them with a repurposed log splitter, and sells them to a scrap metal recycler. Chapter 8 explores the world of social entrepreneurs in more detail.

The following chart outlines some of the differences between social enterprises and social entrepreneurs. The point here is not to argue that one is better than the other but to simply understand their different approaches. They both seek and achieve societal change by focusing on creating markets for solutions.

	SOCIAL ENTERPRISE	SOCIAL ENTREPRENEUR
OWNERSHIP	COMMUNITY	PRIVATE INDIVIDUAL OR SHAREHOLDERS
DISTRIBUTION OF BENEFITS	SURPLUS GOES BACK INTO ENTERPRISE OR COMMUNITY	PROFITS OR DIVIDENDS GO TO OWNERS
MODE OF THINKING	COMMUNITY-BASED ENTREPRENEURIALISM	BUSINESS-ORIENTED ENTREPRENEURIALISM WITH A SOCIAL CONSCIENCE
MODE OF OPERATION	NON-PROFIT (WITH BUSINESS ETHOS)	FOR PROFIT BUSINESS
SCALE	COMMUNITY, LOCALIZED (USUALLY)	SMALL, BIG, OR MULTI-BILLION DOLLAR
CONCENTRATION OF WEALTH	SURPLUSES ARE NOT DISTRIBUTED. RATHER THEY ARE USED TO SUPPORT MANDATE OF NON-PROFIT	INDIVIDUALS CAN GET WEALTHY

GROWING CHANGE: SMALL FARMS ADDRESS BIG PROBLEMS

The small farm movement is a form of social entrepreneurialism that demonstrates an exciting degree of ingenuity and caring. Much more than just businesses, these small farms embody a sense of all around health – health of people, the earth, and communities. This movement offers an opportunity to address fossil fuel consumption, runaway government spending on diseases where diet is the main risk factor, rural depopulation, and even nutrient loading in our water systems. I discuss these problem solvers in Chapter 6.

PROBLEMS	PROBLEM SOLVER EXAMPLES
COSTLY INCARCERATION	SOCIAL ENTERPRISES THAT HIRE REPEAT OFFENDERS
RISING HEALTHCARE COSTS	LOCAL FOOD MOVEMENTS THAT SELL UNPROCESSED FOOD DIRECTLY TO CONSUMERS
CLIMATE CHANGE	SOCIAL ENTREPRENEURS INSTALLING SOLAR ENERGY

GOVERNMENT: FRIEND OR FOE?

Should well-funded government departments solve social and environmental problems? Or should governments just get out of the way so the free market can improve everyone's lot? Neither of those options has a great track record. I see a different role for government. I believe governments can play a vital role in the solutions economy, but that role is outside the traditional ways of thinking about government.

Many societies on Earth face persistent, perennial problems that neither governments nor free markets have been able to meaningfully address in a broad way: ever-growing healthcare costs that put tremendous strain on government budgets, expensive public safety strategies that keep the proverbial revolving doors of prisons spinning, poverty that no one can come close to relegating to history, climate change and other environmental dangers that daunt governments and the public.

I have spent much of my professional life studying, working at, and agonizing over these problems. Over the past decade, I have also seen growing numbers of problem solvers. These are creative people who offer significant solutions to major problems. *The other thing I see, and this is key, is that there are barriers between the problems and the problem solvers.* Those barriers make it very difficult for problem solvers to do their work. *The heart of my message is about connecting the problem solvers with the problems.* That's where governments come in – making an ecosystem in which problem solvers flourish.

You cannot solve a problem without problem solvers. Social enterprises, social entrepreneurs, and the local food movement are all effective and efficient examples of economic ventures that can make the economy work for the most of us.

Before discussing solving some problems in Chapters 4-10, I want to first briefly talk about Canada and how we got to a place of such disparity between Aboriginal peoples and non-Aboriginals. It's important for us all to know where we've been, in order to get to where we need to go.

CHAPTER 3

ECONOMIC RECONCILIATION

RE-IMAGINING INDIGENOUS ECONOMIES

Pretty much everything about Stan McKay is unassuming.

It's a cold January day when I pull into his driveway along Netley Creek about an hour's drive north of Winnipeg. A small camper sits in the yard, a small truck in the driveway. The house is small too, as is the creek next to it. A sign on the deck reads: "Welcome winter!" I am at the right place.

I say that Stan is unassuming, but his life is extraordinary. After residential school he attended a year of teacher's college before becoming a minister in the United Church of Canada. Later, he reluctantly left the congregation in his home community of Fisher River Cree Nation, Manitoba, to take a post as Director of Native Ministries for the national United Church. In 1992, the 500th anniversary of Columbus's "discovery" of North America, Stan became the moderator of the largest protestant denomination in Canada – the first Aboriginal person to take the highest role in any mainline Canadian church.

Along the way, Stan was part of a team that arranged for a national apology for the church's role in the residential school system. In addition, he was involved in setting up self-governance for Aboriginal churches within the national church structure and helped found the Sandy-Saulteaux Spiritual Centre, one of Canada's first Indigenous spiritual training institutions.

But it is the beginning of Stan's story that is perhaps most important. Stan tells me how growing up as a member of Fisher River Cree Nation, about 200 kilometres north of Winnipeg, was near ideal.

The community was self-sufficient. We had cattle, large gardens, and chickens. Plums, pin cherries, raspberries, strawberries, cranberries, and saskatoons grew in abundance. Everyone had

*a root cellar to keep food year round. There were plenty of fish,
geese, and wild game. Even as a child, I knew where my food
came from. I saw how community shared food and life. We
supported each other.*

This gave Stan a solid grounding and a sense of identity and belonging.
But things would change for both Stan and his community. When he was
13, his parents "sent" him to residential school in Birtle, Manitoba. I asked
why his parents *sent* him as I thought residential school was mandatory.

"They didn't have a real choice," he says. "The options had run out
at home." The lake was overfished, and prices paid to Aboriginal fishers
were so low that they often lost money. Settlers had cut down most of
the trees and were taking over the land surrounding the reserve. They
also stole livestock from the people of Fisher River and drained their
lands. This caused flooding on the downstream reserve in spring and
loss of wetlands, which were home to ducks and geese. The unnatural
water fluctuations also killed fur-bearing animals, which eliminated
trapping as an option. Everything seemed stacked against a viable future for the community.

"We couldn't get fair prices for our farm products," Stan says, "because we needed permission from the Indian agent to sell, and that
usually meant a deal for his friends. . . . It was fixed against us from the
start. The captivity was real."

Stan's parents faced a tough decision. "There were no options at
home," he says, "so my parents did the only thing they could, and that
was to send me away."

In *Journey From Fisher River*, a 1994 biography of Stan's life by
Joyce Carlson, his father laments the forced decision:

*I saw the importance of education. . . . It was the only way for
them to avoid enforced dependence. We had always been self-
sufficient. We believed our children had to prepare to live in a
world that was going to be very different. . . . The only way to do
this was through education.*

And so they went. In early September a cattle truck would pull up
and the kids got in the back to the sound of weeping.

In the biography, Stan's sister Pat explains what happened when they reached the big, cold, stone building in Birtle, Manitoba: "I wanted to turn and run. They took all our clothes. They gave us what they called a uniform. We weren't allowed to have anything personal." Pat says that even though she didn't have a term for it at the time she felt the prejudice and racism. "They put us (about 40 girls) in one dorm. There was one toilet and the door was locked from the outside."

Stan tells me that being at the school was like being incarcerated. They were separated from family, from the land, from their cultural teachings, and from their language. It was no place for a child. His parents would scrape money together to pay their kids' fare home for two months each summer. They had to pay in order to see their children.

When I ask Stan if he has ever been back to the school in Birtle, which is still standing, he's blunt: "I have no desire to be on that land again." Many, if not most, of the kids that Stan attended residential school with are either dead, missing, homeless, or they have spent a lot of time incarcerated. Stan fared better than most largely because he was able to spend his first 13 years at home, where he gained a grounding that no school could erase and that would serve him well throughout his life.

Stan's story vividly illustrates the links between reconciliation and the economy.

TRUTH AND RECONCILIATION

In June, 2008, the Prime Minister of Canada, Stephen Harper, made a Statement of Apology to former students of Indian residential schools in the House of Commons and launched the Truth and Reconciliation Commission as part of the Indian Residential Schools Settlement Agreement. The Commission gathered statements from residential school survivors through public and private statement gatherings at various events across Canada. Seven national events, held between 2008 and 2013, commemorated the experiences of former students of residential schools. In the 2015 report of the Truth and Reconciliation Commission, Stan McKay is quoted as saying:

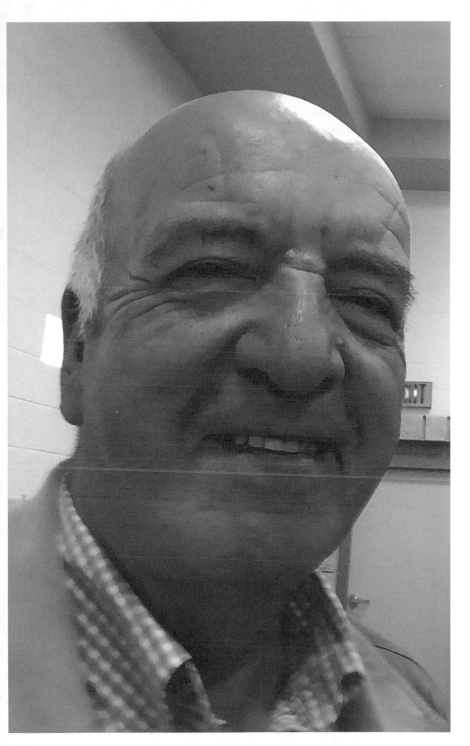

THE VERY REVEREND STAN MCKAY, FIRST ABORIGINAL PERSON TO BECOME MODERATOR OF THE LARGEST PROTESTANT DENOMINATION IN CANADA

[There must be] a change in perspective about the way in which Aboriginal peoples would be engaged with Canadian society in the quest for reconciliation. . . . [We cannot] perpetuate the paternalistic concept that only Aboriginal peoples are in need of healing. . . . The perpetrators are wounded and marked by history in ways that are different from the victims, but both groups require healing.

In my visit with him, I ask him what he means.

The United Church set up a healing fund to address the church's impacts on Aboriginal peoples, but the only people that could apply were Aboriginal – as if only the students and families of residential schools need healing. Our entire country does. Focusing only on the Aboriginal is a denial of the interrelatedness of the history of colonization. If we are to move on, we must move on together.

THE TREATIES

Between 1871 and 1921, the British Crown signed 11 so-called numbered treaties with Indigenous nations. Darcy Wood is the former chief of the Garden Hill First Nation and now the CEO of Aki Energy, a social enterprise we co-founded. On one long road trip, we got into a discussion about the treaties. These agreements were created to allow the Canadian Government to pursue settlement and resource extraction in what is now Manitoba, Saskatchewan, Alberta, and parts of British Columbia, Ontario and the Northwest Territories. With these treaties Canada gained access to immense tracts of land in exchange for a variety of commitments.

Darcy explained to me that people—and not just non-Aboriginal people—have the wrong idea about treaties:

Some of my people think that treaties mean that the government will look after them forever. . . . Some Canadians think that these agreements are the result of a war that Aboriginals lost and so the Aboriginals and their land are conquered. Neither are right.

Darcy says treaties are mutually beneficial arrangements that were supposed to guarantee the welfare of both parties. "Immigrants and their descendants benefit from access to land, free of hassle," he says, "and First Nations were to get the tools they needed to be successful." As Darcy says, we are all treaty people.

Stan looks back at how a misconstrual of the treaty relationship has led to dependence. "My ancestors were told that 'the great white mother' [the Queen] would look after her children," he says. But he says Aboriginal people were ill-equipped for the Queen's adversarial world. Where have we ended up? Instead of the treaties providing the tools Aboriginal people needed for success, as Darcy says, the opposite has happened. This is how Stan puts it:

> Now when someone turns 18, they are entitled to their own welfare cheque. It's an arrival of dependence – a life of low expectations. The dependency is so deeply ingrained. . . . It's almost as though governments are happy to keep us dependent.

Stan recalls a time that predated the concept of unemployment: "Over a generation, social assistance brought dependency. We began to hear the word 'unemployed' – that's a term that was completely unfamiliar to us before."

As for the people lining up for their welfare cheques in a place like Garden Hill, there has to be a better solution than increasing the size of their cheques. Stan agrees by saying he has no energy to advocate for increased welfare rates or housing allowances. "We need to do better," says Stan. "We need to learn again how to take responsibility for our own rights."

"CANADA HAS NO HISTORY OF COLONIALISM"

In September, 2009, less than a year after the residential school apology, Stephen Harper was speaking at a press conference to conclude a meeting of the G20 nations. Part of his remarks included an ill-informed but telling comment that "Canada has no history of colonialism."

Apparently he hasn't spent much time in First Nations communities because evidence of colonialism is everywhere.

Colonialism is the policy or practice of acquiring control over another group's land, then occupying it with settlers and exploiting it economically. In one word, colonialism captures what happened to Stan McKay's community and to Indigenous people overall in Canada.

Peguis First Nation is another example of how the colonial process undermined the local food economy. The people of Peguis farmed fertile reserve land along the Red River north of Winnipeg. In 1907 the Government of Canada held an impromptu meeting with a small number of members of the First Nation where they were plied with liquor and bribed. Canada secured an illegal vote whereby it wrongfully concluded that Peguis agreed to surrender its agriculturally rich land along the Red River in favour of poor agricultural land in Manitoba's Interlake region. Canada and Peguis First Nation have negotiated a settlement for this wrongdoing in the past decade, but the loss of their land and community resulted in the demise of Peguis's local food economy, among other damages that money alone cannot replace.

Many other examples exist of First Nations being confined to unproductive, marginal reserve lands. Interestingly, in the Anishinaabe language, the word for reserve is "*ishkonigan*," which translates as "leftovers." Confinement to reserves often contributed to the collapse of local food economies in part because of the poor quality of the land and in part because the traditional economy relied on a degree of nomadism as people followed seasonal food supplies.

WHERE DOES PRIVILEGE COME FROM?

The Couchiching First Nation, near where I grew up in Northwestern Ontario, further illustrates policies that destroyed a local economy. It is important to understand the process of demise in order to better understand the process of rebuilding. The people of Couchiching once had a sawmill on their reserve. But with the passage of the Indian Act in 1876, it became illegal for the First Nation to sell lumber off-reserve, so the mill was shut down. A non-Aboriginal businessman named J.A. Mathieu took over the sawmill operation and not only made a mint but also left toxic chemicals in the land, a situation that is just now being remediated.

Couchiching First Nation also has several land claims ongoing as a highway, railway, and hydro transmission corridor were put through the First Nation without proper compensation or permission. In addition, a nearby power dam flooded about a quarter of Couchiching's reserve lands, most of it lush farmland, which put an abrupt end to their agricultural history.

All four of my grandparents benefited economically from the demise of the First Nations near them. My paternal grandparents grew up on land that was occupied by the Rainy River First Nation and later owned and operated a grocery store where our neighbours from the Rainy River First Nation would spend most of their social assistance money. My maternal grandparents both grew up on farms in the prairies – my grandfather on land that the Long Plain First Nation thought should be reserve land, not far from the Assiniboine River in central Manitoba. My grandmother grew up near the Qu'Appelle Valley in Saskatchewan. My grandmother's father was a grain farmer. Not only did he have access to land for homesteading, he also had access to markets. For some time after Treaty 4 was signed in 1874, Indigenous farmers in the area did well in terms of production. But Canadian grain buyers wouldn't buy their harvest, claiming unfair competition. So the Aboriginal farmers had to take their wagons to the United States to try and earn income.

The Truth and Reconciliation Commission report reminds us that a key part of the reconciliation process involves those of us who are not Aboriginal becoming aware of our own personal stories and how they connect to the past and current lives of Aboriginal people. Through this we gain a better understanding of the broken spirits among us and the role we must all play on the road to reconciliation.

The Indigenous reality is not an Indigenous problem. It is a Canadian problem. Or, more accurately, it is a Canadian opportunity. As Stan McKay says, reconciliation is a path we must all walk together. One of the most important steps we can collectively take is to create the conditions to allow local economies to re-emerge. They will never be exactly the way Stan McKay described his younger years at Fisher

River, but this book will show how modern local economies can provide jobs, self-worth, hope, and reconciliation.

There was a concerted effort to destroy once-strong local economies. Reconciliation must include the re-emergence of these local economies. Oji-Cree food economy advocate Byron Beardy says it doesn't mean living in teepees and wigwams but rather incorporating Indigenous philosophy into a modern context, in order to "awaken the knowledge and spirit within."

Some Canadians say: "What's done is done. It's time Aboriginal people let go of what happened and move on." Instead, I believe we need to understand exactly what has been done to enable us to think creatively about how to move forward.

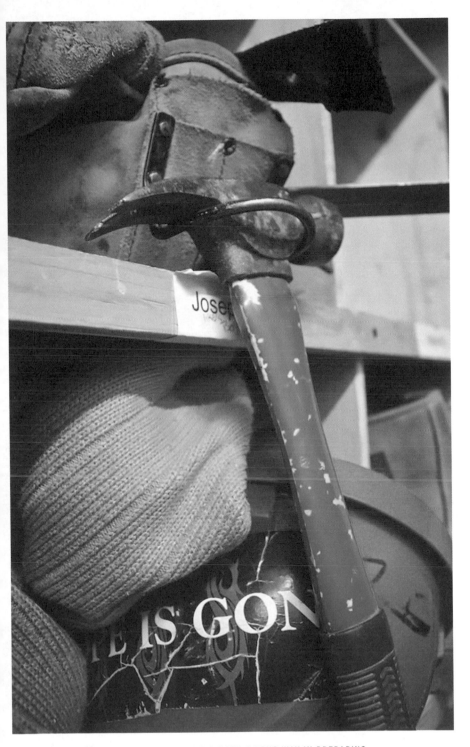

TOOLS OF THE TRADE, OWNERSHIP OF TOOLS GOES A LONG WAY IN PREPARING
FOR THE JOB MARKET.

LET'S SOLVE SOME PROBLEMS

CHAPTER 4

FOOD FOR CHANGE
AN EXAMPLE OF CONNECTING PROBLEM SOLVERS WITH PROBLEMS

For the first time in my life, I was hungry and there wasn't much I could do about it. It was my first visit to the remote Garden Hill First Nation. I was ready to inject a bit of cash into the local economy on my way to fulfilling my most basic needs. I would have loved a sandwich or bowl of soup, or maybe even some local fish.

But I was out of luck. My full wallet was of no use to my empty stomach. There was nowhere on the First Nation to buy a meal.

Of course my situation was different than that of people who lived in the community, but it still demonstrates a gap in the local economy. Actually, it demonstrates the near total lack of a local economy. If an economy can't deliver good food – the most basic necessity – to a hungry visitor with cash in his pocket, it is surely not a functional economy.

Of the 4,000 people living in Garden Hill, about 500 have diabetes. Fifty of those are kids. This is typical for a remote First Nation. According to federal numbers, 17.2 percent of on-reserve adults have diabetes. That's more than three times the national average of 5 percent.

Diabetes is, first and foremost, a health epidemic that exacts a high emotional toll on families and communities. But let's zoom out for a moment to include the economics of diabetes. In 2003, the Manitoba government spent $5.2 million on a six-bed renal hospital in Garden Hill – in today's dollars that's a million dollars per bed. This allowed diabetics to receive dialysis in their community instead of needing to fly out, which is even more expensive and disruptive. On top of the capital expense of the facility in Garden Hill, dialysis costs in the range of $100,000 annually per patient in a remote community. That's an expensive problem.

I see those dollar figures and wonder how much cheaper prevention would be. Is there a way to improve the future health of the community while also creating local employment and saving government money? Could an investment in prevention reap financial and social dividends? What exactly might such an investment look like?

Alice McDougall is an elder who has lived in Garden Hill her whole life. She says diabetes and other diet-related diseases were hardly known as recently as the 1970s. Alice also tells me that when she grew up, gardens were very common in Garden Hill.

Similarly, Dr. Marlyn Cook grew up in Misipawistik Cree Nation in Manitoba. Diabetes was almost unheard of when she was young. She tells me that people ate a lot of moose meat and fish. As "southern food" was introduced and replaced their traditional diet, diabetes took hold.

If you are Aboriginal or know Aboriginal people in Canada, you'll know that diabetes is now woven into their story. The health of Dr. Cook's family paralleled the community's health. Out of her eight sisters, four contracted Type 2 diabetes, causing much family heartache. Today, Dr. Cook, who, in 1987, became the first Indigenous doctor in Manitoba, estimates that more than one out of every three patients she sees is a diabetic, and many of the rest of her clients have diet-related diseases such as high blood pressure and heart disease.

Petey Parisian is a dancer on the powwow circuit in Manitoba. He was 31 when first diagnosed with diabetes. Complications in his left leg led to the amputation of toes, then his foot, then his lower leg, and eventually part of his right foot as well. His aunt has also lost her lower leg to the disease. I say though that Petey *is* a powwow dancer because he still dances. He's inspiring onlookers to stay active.

The extensive literature on diabetes among Indigenous people generally points to a mix of genetic factors (the way in which Indigenous people's bodies had adapted to the traditional diet) and lifestyle factors that account for the high rates of Type 2 diabetes among Indigenous people in Canada and other parts of the world. Key among the lifestyle factors are diet, activity levels, and something I would call general well-being, which is referred to by different researchers as stress, trauma levels, or the like. What is clear is that diabetes came with the switch from an active lifestyle, self-sufficiency, and a country food-based diet to a more sedentary lifestyle and less healthy diet.

NO GARDENS IN GARDEN HILL?

What factors influence diet in a place like Garden Hill? Country foods – a common term for foods hunted, fished, or gathered in the wild – were of course the basis of Indigenous diets not that long ago. They still form a small part of the diet in many places, such as Garden Hill, but have largely been replaced by modern grocery store offerings.

How has this happened? How did the traditional food system and economy give way to modern dependence on grocery supply? The answer is not simple, but let's start by going back to the question of why there are no gardens in a place called Garden Hill (and before long we will return to the economics of diabetes).

Like the Indigenous population in general, Garden Hill has been beat up by a string of government policies and practices. Treaty 5, which Indigenous signatories understood to be a commitment to live together in a good way, was treated by the Crown as a way to get Indigenous people out of the way of white colonial expansion. The Indian Act placed restrictions on cultural practices and commerce, treating Indigenous people in a highly paternalistic fashion.

As I was waiting in the airport of another Northern community, I picked up a copy of the Indian Act lying on a table in the waiting area. According to article 32 (1):

> *A transaction of any kind whereby a band, or a member thereof purports to sell, barter, exchange, give or otherwise dispose of cattle, or other animals, grain or hay, where wild or cultivated, or root crops or plants or their products from a reserve ... to a person other than a member of that band, is void unless the superintendent approves the transaction in writing.*

Stan McKay told me that his parents sold one of their five cows so Stan would have some pocket money when he was away. But this was done only with permission of the Indian Agent and at a cut-rate price. They had to go through him because it was illegal for Indigenous people to sell anything off-reserve without the permission of the Great White Mother's agent. While not enforced in recent years, this restriction was only repealed in 2014.

Combine these oppressive and restrictive forces with the residential schools that shredded the social fabric of communities and with the failure of many successive governments to give meaning to the sharing envisioned in treaties, and you get places like Garden Hill with virtually non-existent formal economies. Into this vacuum came welfare and other forms of dependence.

There is of course a great resilience and beauty in the people of Garden Hill, but there are also deep scars. And the policies that created those scars are not just in the history books. They are in the present.

"THE NORTHERN STORE IS MAKING US SICK"

One form of dependence and exploitation is the North West Company's Northern Store, the Winnipeg-based monopoly retailer located on an island near the Garden Hill reserve. It has replaced the gardens. Like most grocery stores, the Northern Store offers a ready supply of highly processed foods designed primarily for the purpose of corporate profit, not community independence and well-being.

Like most of its suppliers, the North West Company is a publicly traded company with quarterly reports that do not speak of the diabetes epidemic, Northern unemployment, or community well-being but rather focus on shareholder dividends and strategies to maximize profit. They are expected to seek profits, not creative solutions to health problems.

Because places like Garden Hill are only accessible by air for most of the year, costs of food and goods are high. For decades Ottawa has subsidized the shipment of food to remote communities to help reduce costs. The current form of subsidy is the Nutrition North Canada program. The program subsidizes "nutritious" foods flown in and sold up north. The subsidy goes to retailers like the North West Company on a per-pound basis. Qualifying foods cover a wide range of fruits, vegetables, meat, dairy products, eggs, breakfast cereals, and bread products. For 2015-16, the Nutrition North food subsidy budget was $68.5 million, divided amongst about 100 communities. While the program speaks about health, it is more about attempting to level out the gross disparity in affordability between different parts of the country than strategically promoting any sort of health initiative.

TOMATOES ROMA PER
KG

| 1 | PER | 60 | 6060 |

0020408700000   90132654

7 85
NNC

AN EXAMPLE OF AVERAGE PRICE OF FRESH PRODUCE IN REMOTE FIRST NATIONS.

When a subsidy is paid out to either the southern supplier or the northern retailer that subsidy is supposed to be passed on to the consumer but prices remain high. This is likely a result of a lack of competition. As one private grocery store owner pontificated when I shared the approach: "What else do they expect, giving money to a profit-seeking business that holds a monopoly on the market?"

The strategy is an abysmal failure as the incidence of diabetes continues to rise. This should be a surprise to no one as the money is going to monopoly, profit-oriented retailers whose vast majority of sales is unhealthy food. And so diabetes and other diet-related diseases rage on. The federal government has no coherent or realistic plan to address the diabetes epidemic among Indigenous people.

The good news is that problem solvers can solve this problem but first we need to focus on transforming food econcomies. From the perspective of problem solvers, and remembering that there is an "upside to down," we know that:

- dollars that will inevitably be spent on diabetes treatment can be diverted to diabetes prevention now;

- dollars that are being spent now to subsidize the monopoly retailer that sells mostly unhealthy food can be immediately diverted to social enterprises dedicated to selling only healthy food;

- community-minded ventures can create jobs by growing and selling locally (supplemented by imported healthy food) at prices well below what's being charged at the monopoly retailer;

- there is a large local market for food that can be diverted away from the monopoly retailer towards community-minded local businesses;

- there is an obvious potential for gardening in Garden Hill; and

- there is a large untapped source of labour in Garden Hill.

That's a lot of opportunity. And that's why I and my colleagues were in the community in the first place – to discuss with the people the possibility of forming a social enterprise at the intersection of those points of opportunity.

In most places the private sector offers a wide range of goods and services. But that model has limitations that make it less suited than the social enterprise model for places like Garden Hill. Social enterprises also have advantages over chiefs and councils, which often end up running businesses on First Nations. Band councils, after all, are administrative bodies with spotty track records in business. Business is not really their business. Social enterprises can take the market oriented nature of the private sector and combine it with the community focus of the band council.

MEECHIM

In 2014 my co-workers and I at Aki Energy began discussions with the Garden Hill First Nation about setting up a community-based healthy food venture. Out of our talks, Meechim Inc. arose. Meechim is an Oji-Cree word for food. Meechim now runs both a healthy food market and a commercial-sized farm. Meechim is a registered non-profit corporation with a board selected by the community in addition to one member appointed by Chief and Council.

We had asked the First Nation to clear some land thinking a few acres would suffice to get us going. We were amazed to see that they cleared 5.3 hectares (13 acres), similar in size to a large urban shopping mall. It will take some time for the venture to be profitable and to plant the whole area but in year one a fruit orchard was planted, a range of vegetables were grown (potatoes, carrots, beans, peas, and squash), and fencing was erected for 1,000 broiler chickens, laying hens, and turkeys. In 2015, Meechim's first year of operation, ten people were employed for the growing season.

The Meechim healthy food market — another branch of the venture — sells fruit, veggies, meat, healthy cooked meals, and locally caught fish. The market is held at the local TV station with live Oji-Cree language broadcast of what is available. It may be the world's only healthy food shopping channel. Some of the healthy food sold is from the Meechim farm while some is shipped in and sold at rates lower than the Northern Store.

Meechim is also selling healthy food out of the canteen at the arena. It offers fruit, veggies, and Garden Hill chicken soup in place of standard canteen fare. With the help of an innovative foundation called Canadian Feed the Children, we are also working with five classes from the local school. As part of the curriculum, students are gardening and taking the produce home to their families.

I wouldn't want to leave the impression that all this is easy. Changing the status quo can offer its challenges, and we are all learning along the way. But we began to see the benefits immediately.

The goals of Meechim are to improve health in the community, provide employment, and displace many flown-in foods that can be farmed locally. Of course it is also increases overall community capacity to start other economic ventures.

Again, this is not a government program or a charitable endeavour. It is a business. But it is related to government policy, and governments can create conditions that facilitate the re-emergence of the local economy. This is key. *A good idea is not enough if government policies get in the way. The problem solvers and the problems must be connected.*

NUTRITION NORTH SUPPORTS THE AIRLINE INDUSTRY

Governments don't yet understand that it is only strong and healthy local economies that will solve the diabetes problem. They need to focus on supporting problem solvers rather than supporting problem makers. It is obvious that the food subsidy program, as I have described above, is not working to reduce diabetes.

The more offensive problem is that the subsidies are only available for food that is imported. In other words, all the healthy food raised, grown, and sold locally is ineligible for the subsidy. Not only that, ventures like Meechim have to compete against federally subsidized monopoly retailers. Nutrition North Canada subsidies are only available for food that flies!

Whoever designed the subsidy program clearly didn't think that it was possible to garden in places like Garden Hill. The subsidy money goes to monopoly retailers, the airline industry, and fossil fuel companies – instead of to the employment of local people. Such employment would directly benefit the federal government in reduced welfare payments and reduced costs over time for policing, justice, healthcare, and other social services. Employed people are healthier, less likely to get in trouble with the law, less likely to require child welfare intervention, etc.

Then factor in the long-term costs of treating diabetes – just one of several diet-related diseases – or conversely, the potential savings from reducing the incidence of diabetes and the reduced costs of treating diabetics who eat well. Government support for initiatives like Meechim could save governments very significant amounts of money in the long term. And that would be a by-product of healthier, more self-sufficient, more productive communities. That's reconciliation.

GOVERNMENT ROLE

A new role for government is emerging. It can be stated as simply as "making it easy for problem solvers."

In the case of Meechim, the government role could include providing a subsidy equal to Nutrition North – so that ventures like Meechim do not have a rigged disadvantage in relation to the North West Company. "Subsidy" is really the wrong word in this context. Government financial support of social enterprises should be seen more as an investment toward future savings than as a subsidy.

Beyond investment in social enterprises, government support could come in the form of grants or interest-free loans for capital projects (tractors, fences, chicken barns, etc.) as well as operating funds for organizations like Aki Energy that help social enterprises emerge and develop. Building capacity is important, and it requires resources.

It is entirely possible to imagine governments making the supports available to see social enterprises transforming food economies in every diabetes-plagued community. Already in Manitoba alone, there are dozens of First Nations beginning to see local economies re-emerge. Elders are recognizing social enterprises as a modern version of how things used to be done.

Too often governments are quicker to fund problems than solutions. Meechim received a one-time provincial start-up grant of

$300,000, which was equal to the operating costs of providing dialysis to three patients for one year. With the diabetes epidemic on reserves expected to worsen over time, governments have every reason to invest in the solutions economy.

So why aren't there more farms and healthy food markets in diabetes-ravaged communities in Canada? Certainly some of it is because of the lasting legacy of colonization and residential schools, which took away much of the immediate capacity in these communities. But capacity can be regained.

A larger issue is that government policy lags far behind the emerging social enterprise movement. The Nutrition North subsidy is one example. Neither federal nor provincial governments are set up to support the solutions economy.

Again, let me underscore the point that the solutions themselves come not from an office in Ottawa, but from people on the ground who see the upside of down. Ottawa's job is to remove obstacles, connect problem solvers to problems, and redirect monies in ways that make sense over the long term.

NEXT LEVEL

The 13-acre Meechim operation is just a beginning in one place. Take the example of a First Nation with 500 homes, and let's assume each household would buy one chicken a week. This is a local market of 25,000 chickens annually. At $10 a chicken, that's a potential gross revenue of $250,000 for a venture that could supply those chickens. And what about berries, maple syrup, eggs, potatoes, carrots, beets, lettuce, and wild rice? These are all marketable locally.

In a fly-in community, the value of locally produced food would be greatest in the local market. For a First Nation with road access, it might make sense to export some of the food. One example of this is the Flying Dust First Nation in Saskatchewan which grows organic seed potatoes and sells them to eager growers in California. They also operate roadside farmers' markets in the summer and fall. The opportunities are many so long as the problem solvers are connected to the problems.

YOUNG GARDEN HILL FARMER, SHOWING OFF FIRST EGG FROM THE CHICKEN COOP.

CHAPTER 5

POWER UP
ENERGY AND EMPLOYMENT SOLUTIONS
FOR FIRST NATIONS

I grew up near the Rainy River First Nation in Northwestern Ontario. When I'd heard that they had built a 25-megawatt solar farm, I was especially curious to see the project. So I travelled to the First Nation on a cold and sunny day in the winter of 2014.

I wasn't prepared for what I was about to see. Turns out a 25-megawatt solar project is massive. There were 130,000 solar panels, each about a metre by a metre and a half. The project covers about 120 hectares, the equivalent of 200 Canadian Football League fields or about 130 city blocks.

I was joined at the site by Chief Jim Leonard who told me that on that sunny day the project would put $80,000 worth of electricity onto the grid. Over the course of a year, the project is expected to gross about $16 million. Most revenue goes to cover financing of the $160-million venture, with about $1 million left over in annual profits. Chief Leonard says the community has decided to use former Prime Minister Jean Chretien's rule to split the profits three ways. Breaking into a thick francophone accent, Leonard told me "one-tird" would go to future economic development, "one-tird" to education, and "one-tird" back to band members to help them lower their own household utility bills.

I thanked the chief for showing me around and decided to take a drive around the solar farm. Amidst the endless rows of shiny dark panels, a small white flag caught my eye. As I approached it, I saw "Rainy River First Nations" fluttering in the breeze. That's what impresses me most about the project – the Rainy River First Nations developed the project, built the project (completed several months ahead of schedule), and owns the project. I thought to myself, "this is another example of what reconciliation looks like."

MY EXPERIENCE WITH COLONIALISM

And this is where my personal story intersects with that of Rainy River First Nation. Chief Jim Leonard and I have more in common than meets the eye. In 1931 my grandparents started a grocery store in Emo, Ontario, a five-minute drive from the Rainy River First Nation. My dad and uncle bought the store from them in the 1950s, and my brothers bought it from my dad and uncle in the 1980s. The fourth generation is now in the process of taking over. Thanks to the economic opportunity from the store, my family had everything we needed when I was growing up. This gave me every opportunity to do well at school and it put post-secondary education within easy reach. In summers I worked in the store and earned enough money to pay for my university. The lessons I learned about business from working at the store, and from my studies, provided a foundation for the path I am on now.

In 1924, seven years before my grandparents opened the store, government officials removed members of the Rainy River First Nation from six of their seven reserves, all of which were on fertile land on the banks of the Rainy River. First Nation members were placed on one reserve, and the other reserves were developed by non-Aboriginal people. This significantly undermined the First Nation's local food economy, which included hunting, fishing, gathering, and agriculture. Where did they go for their food?

For much of the 85 years my family has run a grocery store in Emo, a major block of customers has been the people of Rainy River First Nation. People who had been self-sufficient were forced to buy food from a store owned by outside interests.

While I am critical of the way in which the Northern Store conveniently stepped in to replace the local food economy in Garden Hill, I have come to realize my own family story is not all that different. I have benefitted greatly from the poverty of others.

Most of us non-Indigenous Canadians, if we admit it, can trace our privilege back to the demise of First Nations. Many of our ancestors settled on ill-gotten land or benefitted from resources to which Indigenous people had legitimate claim. We are part of a system that has worked better for non-Indigenous people than for Indigenous people.

In other words the economy, and society itself, is made for people like me to the exclusion of people who are not like me.

Rainy River First Nation has recently come to an agreement with the governments of Canada and Ontario that compensates them for past wrongs, but not before their agricultural and economic bases were destroyed. This travesty was on top of waves of tuberculosis, residential schools, periods of starvation, and breakdown of families. I was oblivious to all of this growing up just a few miles away. Though one-third of my school class was Anishinaabe, we never learned about what had unfolded in our backyard.

I am grateful for the life-long friends I have at Rainy River First Nation, including Chief Jim Leonard. I am grateful that I have learned more of our shared history. And I am grateful for their solar energy endeavour. The solar farm isn't just a story that belongs to the Rainy River First Nation. It is a story that we can all share. It's a small part of making things right. It is a small step toward reversing a troubling history and building an economy in which everyone matters.

ENERGY GENERATION ON FIRST NATIONS

It is important to understand the sorts of government policies that can create space for an initiative like the Rainy River solar farm and others like it. It is also important to understand the tremendous potential that can be unleashed by such policies.

Rainy River was able to undertake their project because the government of Ontario passed legislation requiring utilities to purchase green power from First Nations at a set, competitive price. The tool used is called a "Feed-in Tariff" or FIT. A tariff, or set price, is paid to people who feed energy back into the electrical grid system. Such prices, when applied to renewable energy, can and should include value for the social and environmental benefits of the power. In the case of a household solar set-up, FIT legislation allows a customer to sell power to the utility when the household has extra and buy from the utility when it is cloudy.

Without FIT legislation, which is relatively common in the United States, utilities tend not to be inclined to buy power from small-scale projects. They usually prefer large-scale, more traditional projects. They need a nudge.

Both small and larger-scale solar energy projects are growing so rapidly in the US that they are a major topic for utilities. One bond-rating agency downgraded the traditional electricity-generation sector as a whole because of the falling cost and widespread availability of solar power.

Governments can encourage these projects by simply requiring utilities, through legislation, to purchase power at reasonable prices – prices that factor in the societal and environmental value and impacts of the power. Without the legislation utilities will be uninterested in buying renewable energy. They much prefer power that can be "dialed up or down" to match the varying demand. This is why most utilities rely on natural gas, coal, and large hydro projects. The argument from the renewable sector is that if the utilities can manage wildly varying demands for power (very cold and very hot days require more electricity than mild days), then surely they can manage varying supplies of power from renewable sources.

I now live in Winnipeg, which is only a three-hour drive from the Rainy River First Nation. Until recently there was no policy framework to support solar development. There are two large wind farms, but they are owned by outside interests. The towers and blades were manufactured outside of Canada, so not only do the profits leave the province, the manufacturing jobs also went elsewhere.

On a clear day, members of the Swan Lake First Nation, in Manitoba, can see one of those large wind farms, a 120-megawatt (MW) project owned by Ontario-based Algonquin Power. Though Swan Lake First Nation has wanted a wind farm for over a decade, in the absence of government legislation that would make it possible, all they can do is watch someone else's turbines spin in the distance.

The 120-MW wind farm near the Swan Lake First Nation required a $240 million investment. Projects of that size lie beyond the financial reach of most First Nations. It would have been smarter if Manitoba had brought in legislation to require its utility, Manitoba Hydro, to purchase power from community-sized wind and solar projects, which are more easily financed and have a greater local economic impact for the invest-ment. In fact, Hydro could even loan First Nations the money to build community-sized projects and be paid back out of the revenue generated.

In 2006, researchers from the University of Minnesota, led by Dr. Arne Kildegaard, studied the impact of a 10.5-MW community-owned wind project compared to a corporately owned project of the same size. Their analysis supported an increasing body of research in-dicating that community ownership is the most important factor in maximizing local benefits. They concluded that community-owned projects return five times the benefits of similarly sized, corporately controlled projects.

Both wind and solar are relatively low-risk investments if a buying price is set. This makes them both a great fit for community ownership.

Community-owned solar and wind-power projects are blossom-ing in North Dakota, Minnesota, and Ontario, but there are none in Manitoba. The difference is not in wind or solar resources. If anything Manitoba has better average solar and wind resources than its neigh-bours. The difference is government legislation. Manitoba's neighbour-ing jurisdictions decided to make it easy for problem solvers and are reaping the rewards of rural revitalization, reduced greenhouse gas (GHG) emissions, and revenue generation.

Encouraging small-scale production is a faster, less risky way to ad-dress growing energy demand than mega-projects that require years to plan and build and require massive capital expenditures. And again, the local economic benefits would be greater.

Manitoba Hydro has recently announced a program that will pay for about 25 percent of the upfront cost of a solar project. Social enter-prises are encouraged by this. It will be interesting to see what develops.

MAKING IT EASY FOR PROBLEM SOLVERS: REDUCING ENERGY CONSUMPTION ON FIRST NATIONS

Let's turn from energy generation to energy efficiency, another oppor-tunity for social enterprises. Mervin Murdock is the general manager of Fisher River Builders, a construction company owned by the Fisher River Cree Nation, about 200 kilometres north of Winnipeg. Up until

FIRST NATIONS WOULD ALSO BE GREAT PLACES
FOR SOCIAL ENTERPRISE CENTRES, MODELLED
AFTER THE SOCIAL ENTERPRISE CENTRE IN
WINNIPEG'S NORTH END. HERE, MORE LOCAL
COMMUNITY-WEALTH CREATING BUSINESSES COULD
BE INCUBATED SUCH AS A FISH EXPORT CO-
OP, A SMALL MOTEL, A USED CLOTHING STORE,
A WILD RICE PROCESSING COMPANY, A COFFEE
SHOP, A HAIR SALON, AND SO ON. THE SOCIAL
ENTERPRISE CENTRE IN WINNIPEG CONTINUES
TO ESTABLISH NEW SOCIAL ENTERPRISES ON AN
ANNUAL BASIS. EXISTING SOCIAL ENTERPRISES
THERE WORK TOGETHER TO ENSURE THERE IS
THE MANAGEMENT AND BUSINESS EXPERTISE
TO MAKE NEW VENTURES A SUCCESS.

a few years ago, Fisher River Builders focused almost entirely on building a few new homes a year. Now Murdock runs the largest residential geothermal company in Western Canada, and it's a First Nations social enterprise. Aki Energy is proud to have had a role in its establishment. Murdock tells me that the community members and homeowners are very proud of his highly trained crews.

Geothermal systems – otherwise known as ground source heat pumps – use warmth from underground to heat buildings in the winter and the coolness underground in summer to keep buildings cool. A biodegradable fluid is pumped through about 600 metres of plastic pipe, which is buried in trenches below the frost line (about 2.1 metres down) near the house. Down there, even if it is minus 20 degrees outside, the temperature is plus 4. This warms the fluid, which is pumped back into a unit in the house that makes that warmth available for space heating by means of a compression process. While the system uses some electricity, it uses far less energy than typical forms of heating and cooling.

In summer the same system cools the house by "dumping" heat into the ground. Manitoba Hydro estimates that it costs only $20 to provide air conditioning throughout the entire summer to homes that had no cooling before. On one particularly hot July day, an Elder happily phoned the band office to leave a message: "Tell the Chief it's so cool at my place that you can hang meat in here!"

At Fisher River, the cost of installation in an existing home is about $18,000, depending on location, soil conditions, and house conditions. The reduction in monthly energy costs is significant.

Fisher River Builders have retrofitted 175 homes in three years, about one-third of the 500 homes on the First Nation. They have also started commercial projects, installing geothermal systems in the local fitness centre, health centre, and car wash. They will soon be taking on work mentoring other First Nations and working in other communities in their area.

Geothermal is a good option for many First Nations because it cuts space heating costs by up to 75 percent, usually replacing expensive electrical heat. Large lots and collectively owned land on reserves also make it easier to find good places to bury the piping loops. Doing

FISHER RIVER BUILDERS INSTALLING GROUND LOOPS FOR GEOTHERMAL HEATING SYSTEMS.

many systems in one place is also more economical, with per-unit savings of about 33 percent compared to installing a single system. The technology is also a good fit for First Nations because it is labour intensive, providing employment where it is badly needed.

A typical First Nation home heated with electricity will require about $3,600 a year for space and water heating as well as powering appliances and lights. This means that for every 500 homes, there is roughly $1.8 million a year leaking out of the community. Add the energy used in commercial and community buildings like arenas, nursing stations, and schools, and the total leakage is easily $2.5 million a year. If rate increases are considered, this can quickly amount to $30 million over a decade. This is money that creates virtually no local employment and is unavailable to be spent on other priorities such as healthy food or new housing.

If geothermal were installed in all these buildings, it would cost approximately $12 million but would reduce space-heating costs by $30 million or more over the life cycle of the equipment, leaving plenty of net bill savings.

BRINGING FUTURE SAVINGS FORWARD

What is the policy climate that makes Fisher River Builders possible? In 2012, the Manitoba government passed its Energy Savings Act which made provision for "on-bill financing" for any energy-efficiency project that would pay for itself within its expected lifespan. That means that if an $18,000 geothermal system will save the customer more than $18,000 over its expected lifetime, Manitoba Hydro will put up the $18,000. The utility then adds a financing fee to the customer's monthly bill to regain its capital expenditure.

At Fisher River, the geothermal systems typically save customers $150 or more per month on their electrical bills ($1800 per year). The average monthly financing fee is about $100. So from month one, there is a net saving of about $50 for the household each month, and the household has no capital cost, just a lower bill each month. The Manitoba Hydro on-bill financing program is aptly called Pay As You Save (PAYS).

INSULATION TECHNICIANS WARMING UP HOMES IN WINNIPEG TO REDUCE HEATING BILLS.

The utility continues to charge the fee until it has recovered its initial expenditure. The benefit to the utility is reduced overall electrical demand, which frees up more power for sale, delays the need for expensive new generation, and helps them expand their services to groups that utilities call "hard-to-reach customers."

PAYS is a tool that brings future savings forward to the present so there are resources to invest in solutions. The Manitoba government set the conditions for First Nations, in collaboration with the utility, to solve a problem, and First Nations are jumping at the chance.

Those of us in the social enterprise sector lobbied hard for the Energy Savings Act, which includes the PAYS provision. Social enterprises identify waste in the economy and turn that waste into a resource. In this case the waste identified is the wasted energy of inefficient heating systems. Some of the money that went out of the community to pay for that wasted energy is redirected toward local employment. Some of the money is simply saved, making households and the larger economy more efficient.

The opportunity for training and employment is another benefit of this particular social enterprise. Fisher River Builders obtained the training that Aki Energy offers and does the work, rather than some outside contractor. The labour component of project spending can re-circulate in the local economy.

Aki Energy served as social enterprise incubator. We were involved at the ground level – first lobbying for the Energy Savings Act, then working with Fisher River on project-management and business-development skills through courses and mentorship. We also facilitated training and were involved in negotiating the agreement with Manitoba Hydro.

We are just beginning. In 2015 the Fisher River Cree Nation and the Peguis First Nation, in Manitoba, signed agreements with Aki Energy and Manitoba Hydro to complete an additional $14 million worth of geothermal systems. These First Nations now own the two largest residential geothermal companies in Western Canada. And they are both social enterprises, operated for the benefit of the community.

Sagkeeng First Nation and Long Plain First Nation, also in Manitoba, have collectively installed nearly a million dollars worth of geothermal technology in their first year. We hope to see $100 million worth of geothermal systems installed on Manitoba First Nations in the next decade. Thinking more broadly, geothermal installations in 100,000 First Nation homes in Canada could result in roughly $1.5 billion in capital investment, $750 million in labour, 15,000 person-years of employment, and $5 billion in reduced utility bills over 20 years.

The federal government has an incredible opportunity to lower utility bills on First Nations in both new homes that are being built and existing homes that can be retrofitted.

The Canadian Mortgage and Housing Corporation (CMHC) funds new-home construction on First Nations. Their policy is generally to keep the upfront costs to a minimum, and extras are not usually allowed. For example a new home can be hooked up to geothermal technology for an additional $5,000 (installation in a new home is cheaper than retrofitting an existing home), a move that would cut energy bills by about $1,800 a year. But CMHC won't allow it because they see the $5,000 as a cost rather than an investment. They can't afford to save money.

Indigenous and Northern Affairs Canada (INAC) is responsible for upkeep of existing homes and also pays operating costs – including utility bills – of all social assistance clients on First Nations either directly or indirectly. Despite high bills across the country, INAC has no comprehensive strategy to reduce bills. They should offer to finance any and all guaranteed bill-reduction measures. Instead of paying for wasted energy, they could be saving money through reduced bills and through employment, which takes people off their social assistance rolls. They have an opportunity to spend money on solutions rather than problems. Instead the government chooses not to save money and to avoid creating jobs for First Nations.

GOVERNMENT GETS IN THE WAY

Through this whole process, we had to fight our way through many outdated federal rules and regulations that caused great inconvenience and difficulty. The federal government actually declared the financing fee (the on-bill charge to pay back the upfront investment in geothermal) as an ineligible expenditure for people on social assistance whose

LEARNING AND TEACHING THE TOOLS OF THE TRADE IN FISHER RIVER.

utility bills are covered by federal programs. They preferred to pay the higher bill that created no employment instead of the guaranteed-by-law lower bills that created employment.

Shortly after we signed an $8 million partnership agreement with Waywayseecappo First Nation in western Manitoba, we received a phone call from INAC. They were not allowing us to work with any more First Nations because they didn't want their social assistance money being used to pay the financing fee. They made this ruling knowing that net bills would decrease – the electricity savings outweigh the financing fee – and that jobs would be created. We have found out that very few people in the system have the authority to change rules, no matter how ridiculous they are, and these people are inaccessible to problem solvers.

Aki took to the media to get our story out. An expected phone call came from the minister's office with an offer to restore our funding. They seemed surprised when I told them we didn't have *any* funding. A subsequent call came hinting at an offer of $8 million to do geothermal at Waywayseecapo First Nation. We frustratingly declined the money. Why? Because it would have been unfair to the four First Nations who were already paying the financing fee. And because it seemed INAC was reluctant to embrace a vision that could create significant change for hundreds of First Nations.

The reason why they offered the money is because this way they can maintain control. We often hear that INAC is a colonial department. This is a good example. Force the high-cost, low-impact approach so that they can maintain control. Apparently, this is preferable to the low-cost, high impact approach that gives communities the tools they need to be successful.

The other problem with INAC's preferred approach is that it deviates greatly from Aki's strategy of training local band members to run their own social enterprise and to do their own installing and maintenance. Their preferred approach is to do what one industry insider summarized to me in an acronym as DBBO – "design, build, and bugger off." The $8 million in funding would almost certainly have to go to tender. Several companies would likely respond with the lowest bidder getting the job. That lowest bidder would win the bid by importing labour and installing cheap equipment. The equipment would have less than desirable efficiencies and likely fail after a few years. At that point, expensive outside contractors would have to be brought in to try to get the systems up and running. Ask anyone who lives on a First Nation and they will tell you, whether its water systems, housing, or energy – this is common procedure.

Ottawa should instead be partnering with First Nations – which requires an ongoing relationship – and offering to finance any proven and reliable energy-saving technologies that offer up enough savings to pay back the upfront costs over time. We're not talking just about geothermal energy. Depending on the context, solar may work or even biomass.

BIOMASS: LIKE THE GOOD OLD DAYS

Aki Energy's management team, including Darcy Wood, Kate Taylor, and me, visited a Manitoba Hutterite colony that had replaced an expensive propane heating system with an efficient biomass alternative. More than a dozen Manitoba Hutterite colonies are now burning wood chips to heat water that is circulated through underground pipes and then used to heat the 50 or so buildings on each colony.

Darcy, a former chief, noted that there are many similarities between First Nations and Hutterite Colonies. Most importantly, the land is collectively owned. Leadership can make decisions that can end up making community-wide installations easy, and retrofitting an entire community, rather than a few buildings, lowers the upfront cost and increases the benefits of the system.

This sort of system would be particularly sensible in remote communities that ship in diesel fuel over winter roads for their space-heating needs. The costs and inefficiencies are outrageous, and the government, which pays for it, willingly pours money into the problem. Diesel fuel that has travelled thousands of kilometres from its original source is shipped in at great expense to governments and First Nations and considerable profit to outside entities. I have not yet met any Canadian who would argue with our approach of using local social enterprise labour to harvest wood from right around the communities.

Over the past 20 years, the Cree at Oujé-Bougoumou, in Quebec, have built a district biomass system that provides heat to over 140 homes and 20 public buildings on their First Nation. They are very happy with their biomass operation, but it hasn't yet caught on across Canada because of an outdated federal approach to providing heat on First Nations. If a community of 500 homes were given the opportunity to combine energy generation and energy efficiency, it could install a 10-MW wind or solar project – presuming it were close enough to the grid and in a jurisdiction with a Feed-in Tariff policy – and receive annual revenues of $2.5 million with a payback of 10 to 12 years. With a federal government PAYS system, it could also install a centralized biomass boiler system to heat the 500 homes as well as public buildings. This would create a market for nearly $1 million of locally and sustainably harvested biomass annually. Most of that money would go toward wages.

PAYS systems and FITs are good examples of policies that connect problem solvers to problems. They are proven to work. If put in place, widespread adoption will follow.

NEXT LEVEL

In her 1969 book, *The Economy of Cities*, Jane Jacobs writes about the economic importance of businesses expanding into new lines that are only partially related to the old. This happens when geothermal installers turn their skills to installing solar water-heating units. It happens when a First Nation-owned coffee shop develops its own coffee brand to sell to other First Nations or when a small, local fish co-op turns an annual local harvest into a value-added boxed product. This is how creative economies grow, and it's no different on First Nations. All the examples given in this book are seeds that can grow and adapt and reinvent themselves and spawn related ventures.

Aside from high utility bills and high food prices on First Nations, there are other opportunities masquerading as problems. In many remote communities, there are many derelict vehicles. In the Garden Hill First Nation, it is estimated that there are 5,000 of these vehicles littered throughout the community. An initial assessment determined that these cars are worth $300 each, or $1.5 million. Even if it cost

$300 to ship the cars to a crusher, and even if it didn't turn a profit, such a venture could create some employment.

There are jobs to be created on First Nations. Lots of them. Governments need to expand upon successes like Rainy River First Nation and Fisher River Cree Nation. Governments need to set the conditions. First Nations are waiting.

CHAPTER 6

GROWING SOLUTIONS
DIVERSIFYING THE FOOD SYSTEM
TO CURB HEALTH AND OTHER COSTS

I consider small farms and the local food movement to be key parts of the solutions economy. When I visit a small farm, I feel the energy of something more than just a business. As the number of traditional farmers continues its decades-long decline, the number of small-scale, low-input social entrepreneurial farms continue to grow. These farmers are problem solvers who not only provide quality food but also reduce greenhouse gas emissions, diversify rural economies, and reduce healthcare costs. Their great potential could be unleashed if governments would create space for them.

First I want to briefly look at six problems that the small farm movement helps to solve, remembering, of course, that problems are the flip side of opportunities. The six problems relate to health, profit motives, rural depopulation, nutrient loading, climate change, and labour practices.

1. DOUBLE-DOUBLE EQUALS TRIPLE TROUBLE
I think many Canadians know on some level that our collective diet has to change. We're surrounded by bad options, and too often we choose them.

The percentage of Canadians with weight problems has doubled in the past 30 years. According to Statistics Canada, in 2014 over 14 million Canadians self-reported as being overweight or obese. More importantly the number of Canadians with diet-related diseases is five million and growing. Diet-related diseases account for four of the six leading causes of death in Canada. That doesn't mean that if we all avoided doughnuts and Coke, no one would get cancer, heart disease, or diabetes or have strokes, but it does mean we're eating our way to the hospital. The societal costs of this are tremendous.

According to the Canadian Diabetes Cost Model, the healthcare costs of treating diabetes are $3 billion annually. If you add in costs to employers in sick time, health insurance premiums, and costs incurred by patients, the number balloons to an estimated $13.8 billion. Though specific cost break downs are not available for cancer, heart disease, and stroke, I estimate that 75 percent of health budgets go toward treating diseases for which diet is a major risk factor. I find that staggering. But I find it even more troubling that the same governments that bend under the weight of health budgets subsidize and play along with a food system that makes us sick.

The pressure of healthcare costs – which make up about 40 percent of provincial budgets on average – is putting constant strain on governments. In 2011, David Dodge, the former Governor of the Bank of Canada, predicted that if trends continue, healthcare spending would take up 80 percent of provincial budgets by 2030. A food system tilted toward consumption of foods loaded with sugar, salt, fat, and carbs is largely to blame.

The food industry spends millions to research taste. In large part the intent is to increase profits by preying on our weaknesses for sugar, salt, fat, and carbs. They understand our taste physiology and psychology much better than we do. Then they spend billions on advertising to various age groups to lure us in. Not only are we surrounded with bad choices, we are bombarded by them.

2. FOR-PROFIT FOOD

Of course the food industry, like all industries, is just trying to make money. In one sense that is fair. But does it make sense to hand responsibility for your family's diet – the stuff they put in their bodies every day to keep them alive – to companies whose primary responsibility is to satisfy the financial self-interest of shareholders?

Farmers, grocers, and all the players in between have always sought to make a good living. And surely there has always been some tension between doing what is most profitable and doing what is healthiest and safest for the consumers and land. But with the consolidation in the food and agriculture sector, the profit motive has gone into overdrive. Fewer and fewer, bigger and bigger companies control production, wholesaling, processing, and retailing. The same is true of companies that sell agricultural inputs such as fertilizers, pesticides, seed, and livestock feed and supplements. For a decade, six companies have controlled 75 percent of the global pesticide and high-tech seed business. If current merger talks succeed, it is entirely possible that three companies will control 65 percent of pesticide sales and about 60 percent of commercial seed sales.

This system provides food that is, generally, inexpensive (not counting health and environmental costs), visually appealing, durable in transport, and relatively long-lasting on the shelf. But the primary responsibility of the people who make decisions about our food – leaders of massive companies – is to shareholders. Of course, sometimes they promote healthy food as that has become a profitable niche, but to a troubling extent they have us eating greasy food right out of their hands.

The shareholders of the companies that feed us aren't thinking about whether your kids have a healthy breakfast, whether you are at risk of getting diabetes, whether farm soils are thriving, or whether agricultural workers are making a good living for their families. They're thinking about stock value. The fundamental goal of these companies is to make money, and often that means that their goal is to put as much sugar, fat, and salt into your body as possible.

Unfortunately, to a considerable extent consumers are hooked on this system. We are addicted to cheap, attractive food that tickles the most fickle of our taste buds. That's why we keep eating stuff that kills us, and that's why healthcare providers endlessly tell us to eat better.

A caveat is required. The food sector is broad and still somewhat diverse. There are farmers, grocers, and restauranteurs who maintain a strong sense of social contract with eaters. And even the large companies do the right thing at times.

Advocates of change to the current food system often focus their attention on farmers. They are an easy target. And while farmers bear a great responsibility to care for the land that is both private property and a resource essential for the common good, and while there are troubling aspects of common farming practices, the food system is much bigger than just farmers. Ultimately consumers and farmers need to work together.

3. A TASTE FOR OIL

The Manitoba Department of Agriculture lists all inputs purchased by farmers on an annual basis. In 2013, Manitoba farmers spent $2.4 billion on inputs. About 13 percent of that was spent on fuel. Another 27 percent went toward fertilizer, the production of which relies heavily on natural gas. Sixteen percent was spent on pesticides, which again require considerable amounts of fossil fuel to produce. And another 4 percent went toward heating and electricity. Further energy is required to process, store, and transport food.

The breakdown will vary from one jurisdiction to another as agricultural practices vary considerably across regions, but everywhere, a significant portion of every dollar spent on food ultimately goes to cover the energy required to grow, process, store, and transport the food. While estimates of that portion vary depending on the assumptions made, Dale Allen Pfeiffer, in his 2006 book, *Eating Fossil Fuels*, estimates that energy comprises as much as 90 percent of the cost of food from our present system. Imagine a little exhaust pipe sticking out the side of your plate. This over-reliance on fossil fuels is a significant factor contributing to climate change.

In Manitoba, the agricultural sector accounts for about 30 percent of provincial greenhouse gas emissions. Nationally the figure is 10 percent. Again, this is not to wag a finger at farmers, it is to acknowledge that we all need to work together to figure out how to eat less oil.

MANITOBA FARM EXPENDITURES IN 2013	
FERTILIZER (NATURAL GAS)	$644 MILLION
PESTICIDES (OIL)	$373 MILLION
MACHINERY FUEL (MOSTLY DIESEL)	$310 MILLION
ELECTRICITY AND HEATING FUEL	$103 MILLION
COMMERCIAL FEED AND SEED (HALF OF COMMERCIAL FERTILIZERS IN CANADA ARE USED ON THESE CROPS AND THEREFORE FOSSIL FUELS ARE BURIED IN THIS STAT)	$976 MILLION

4. INDENTURED LABOUR

Canada's food system is dependent on temporary and seasonal workers from other countries. The meat, fruit, and vegetable sectors would be in crisis if they had to rely on Canadian citizens to do the work required. Meat-packing plants would have to shut down or pay far higher wages. Fruit and vegetable farms would face the same dilemma.

Meat packing plants rely on the Temporary Foreign Worker Program, which brings in workers from other countries and gives them a pathway to citizenship if they stay on the job for two years. Some call it a modern form of indentured labour. Turnover in these plants, past the two-year stay, is high. The work is non-unionized, low-pay, unpleasant, highly repetitive, and often very hard on people's health.

Many large fruit and vegetable operations rely on the Seasonal Agricultural Worker Program, which brings in workers from Mexico and the Caribbean for a maximum of eight months per year. These workers are not allowed to bring their families with them, and the program does not include a pathway to citizenship or permanent residency.

These people are considered good enough to pick our peaches but not good enough to be our neighbours. Some of these workers have spent eight months a year in Canada for 20 years or more. They are not allowed to switch employers, and if they cause any troubles, their employers may not request them back the next year. Canadians simply won't do the hard physical labour these workers do, yet our meals depend on them.

5. RURAL DEPOPULATION

Another thing that is happening in the food system is the decrease in the number of farmers. Since 1981 the number of farms in Manitoba has shrunk by a third. The average size of farms has increased significantly. These trends continue both in Manitoba and elsewhere. This is changing the complexion of rural Canada. While some rural communities thrive, many are in decline. This consolidation of agricultural landholdings is very much a part of the larger consolidation happening in the food system. For the most part, bigger farms work in a sort of unspoken collaboration with the larger food system.

6. NUTRIENT LOADING

Here in Manitoba we hear much about the deeply troubled state of Lake Winnipeg, Canada's "other Great Lake," as we sometimes call it. Excess nutrients in the water, which cause dangerous algae blooms, are one of the main problems. Some of those nutrients come from urban sewage systems, but many of them come from synthetic agricultural fertilizers that get washed into waterways.

BIG PROBLEMS, SMALL PROBLEM SOLVERS

Amidst a food system that, in many ways, just doesn't make sense, problem solvers are emerging. Small-scale, low-input, localized farmers are offering a fundamentally different kind of food. These farmers and their customers simply opt out of the massive tangle of the heavily consolidated, energy-intensive, high-input food system.

Kalynn Spain is the founder and coordinator of Small Farms Manitoba. She was interested in starting her own small farm, so she decided to visit some. In the first growing season, she went to 80 farms. She realized a network was needed. Small Farms Manitoba now "connects eaters with farmers from across the province." Spain estimates the number of small, low-input, direct-market oriented farms in Manitoba is 300 and growing.

The term "small farm" is admittedly a bit loose. Generally it refers to diverse farming operations that have some vegetables and most likely a range of animals. Some also grow grain. Some are organic, and some are not, but most seek to minimize outside inputs, preferring manure over commercial fertilizers and limiting reliance on large energy-intensive machinery. Many sell directly to customers, either through farmers' markets, micromarketing networks (a truck that goes from several farms to a nearby population centre regularly), farm gate sales, or similar mechanisms. Small farms operate largely, though not always entirely, outside the standard food and agriculture system, bypassing the multinational ag companies and the huge wholesalers and retailers.

Each small farm looks different, but the one run by Marilyn Firth and Bruce Berry is fairly typical. They both left behind professional jobs in Southern Ontario – Marilyn as a TV producer and Bruce as an engineer – in 2007. They moved west and founded Almost Urban Vegetables on the outskirts of Winnipeg. Coming up on their eighth season, they now deliver food to 70 families in the city. They also sell eggs, chicken, and lamb at the local farmers' market. All of this is done on just 1.6 hectares (four acres) of land, with no imported fertilizers or pesticides.

In some ways this form of farming is a return to something that looks more like farms from two or three generations back, but it also involves a great deal of modern innovation. Small farmers are constantly experimenting with a range of techniques and technologies. They tend to be highly adaptive and entrepreneurial.

While it is difficult to measure the economic impact of the small-scale food sector, there are some numbers available, as an example, for Manitoba. According to government numbers, gross sales from the entire food and beverage industry are worth $4.6 billion annually (2011), representing an estimated 28 percent of the provincial manufacturing output. Within the small-scale food sector, the value of direct sales was estimated to be between $65 and $79 million in 2012. In addition, farmers' market sales in Manitoba have been estimated to be approximately $240 million per year and growing.

But the small farm movement is as much about an ethos as it is about dollar figures, specific sets of practices, or clearly defined size limits. Financial viability is, of course, important for small farmers, but they are also motivated by the satisfaction of providing healthy food, connecting directly with consumers, watching the land thrive, and working hard. The small farm ethos is about healthy living, and thus it serves as preventative and proactive healthcare. It is geared toward minimally processed foods grown with limited additives. It nurtures and promotes health consciousness among its customers.

It is also about minimizing off-farm inputs such as energy and synthetic fertilizers. While small farmers still require varying amounts of fossil fuel energy in various forms, their style of raising food reduces greenhouse gas emissions compared to standard food and agriculture systems.

BIG AG MODEL	SMALL FARM MODEL
LARGE NUMBER OF ACRES	SMALL NUMBER OF ACRES
PRODUCT SOLD TO GLOBAL MARKETS	PRODUCTS SOLD INTO LOCAL MARKETS
HIGH GROSS RECEIPTS	LOW GROSS RECEIPTS
LESS DIVERSITY IN CROP AND LIVESTOCK	MORE DIVERSITY IN CROP AND LIVESTOCK
SOIL DEPLETING	SOIL BUILDING
FERTILIZERS ARE USUALLY IMPORTED AND SYNTHETIC - MADE WITH FOSSIL FUELS	FERTILIZERS ARE MORE OFTEN NATURAL AND SOURCED FROM ON FARM
FOOD IS BROUGHT TO THE LIVESTOCK AS IS COMMON WITH FEEDLOTS	LIVESTOCK IS GRASS FED AS MUCH AS POSSIBLE - LIVESTOCK IS MOVED TO THE FOOD
FOOD USUALLY SOLD TO LARGE COMPANIES FOR "VALUE ADDED" PROCESSING (SUCH AS MILK TO CHEESE SLICES AND WHEAT TO SUGAR LADEN CEREALS)	FOOD USUALLY SOLD UNPROCESSED, DIRECTLY TO CONSUMERS

Small farms also reverse the trend of rural depopulation, providing families with income from relatively small parcels of land. In an age of growing farm-sizes and massive capital costs, it is hard for children of farmers to stay in agriculture, and it is nearly impossible for new farmers to enter the industry. The small farm model provides another option, allowing more people to farm. This diversification of the agricultural sector can only be good for the economy and for rural communities. The loose social contract between urbanites and food producers benefits from thriving and diverse rural communities.

Finally, small farms ensure that no labourers are treated unfairly along the food chain and also that harmful agricultural runoff is reduced or eliminated.

Small farms will not replace the vast fields of wheat, canola, corn, beans, and other crops in Canada's farming regions. But why couldn't a province like Manitoba produce a large portion of its own vegetables at least in the growing season? And why couldn't Manitoba be entirely self-sufficient in things like garlic, onions, cabbage, squash, and other vegetables that store well?

Remember, small farms are not just a different form of production, they are a step outside the entire food and agriculture system. Think of local baked potatoes from a farmer you know instead of french fries designed to benefit shareholders. Think of homemade local roast chicken instead of frozen chicken fingers with a list of unpronounceable ingredients. In the small farm model, the money spent goes straight to nearby families rather than distant shareholders. It is an investment in solutions. The food is less processed. The impact on the land is less. Labour practices are just. Runoff is reduced. Health costs are reduced. And greenhouse gas emissions are reduced. Yet the subsidies go elsewhere, and the policies create obstacles.

MAKING IT EASIER FOR PROBLEM SOLVERS

What role does government policy play? Between 1986 and 2010, federal farm subsidies ranged between $6 and $8 billion annually. In 2011 subsidies and indirect transfers accounted for 14 percent of gross farm receipts. In Manitoba alone large farmers, in a typical year, receive $280 million in direct farm support.

One form of support is a direct fuel subsidy. In many jurisdictions farm fuel receives a direct subsidy (in the form of lower taxes than are charged for non-farm fuel), but reducing fossil fuel use is not incentivized. The more GHGs you emit, the more you benefit.

While it makes no sense that these subsidies give large farms an unfair, taxpayer-funded advantage over small farms, the solutions economy is not about simple subsidies. The answer to the food-system problems is not to simply shift subsidies. More creative and effective options exist.

Consider the example of the University of Winnipeg, which contracted with a local social enterprise, Diversity Foods, to run and transform the university's food services. Diversity buys over half its food from about three dozen Manitoba small farms. This is healthy, unprocessed, whole food. Diversity also ditched its deep fryers in favour of healthier methods of food preparation.

What if all government institutions did the same? Government-funded and government-run institutions are the largest buyers of food in Canada. Hospitals, care homes, jails, government offices, and schools have huge food budgets. What if governments, following the lead of the University of Winnipeg, devoted just 20 percent of their food budgets to purchasing food from small farmers? This would create space for the small farm sector to flourish, creating efficient distribution systems and driving further innovation in terms of production techniques and technologies.

I estimate that, in Manitoba, public kitchens serve about 300,000 meals per day. At about $1.50 per meal, that adds up to $150 million worth of purchasing power over a year. That money can go toward reducing healthcare costs, reducing GHG emissions, and revitalizing rural areas, or it can go to buying processed foods from far away. It makes no sense for a hospital to serve pizza in its cafeteria and treat cardiac patients an elevator ride away.

WHAT ABOUT?...

There are two common concerns about requiring public kitchens to purchase food from small farms. The first is cost. The standard food system achieves low cost through scale, low wages, and externalization of environmental and social costs. That is, if the health and environmental costs of that system were actually included, the prices would be higher.

The higher costs of food from small farms can be mitigated by allowing institutions to fulfill much of their 20 percent requirement in seasons when local food is more readily available and less expensive. Costs of small farm food could also be expected to drop over time as a robust market would result in some efficiencies and greater scale. There may indeed be some cost increases, but if there were a 20 percent premium on 20 percent of the food purchased, the overall cost is bumped up by only 4 percent. Over time these costs would be more than recovered in reduced healthcare expenditures.

The Public Health Agency of Canada estimates that getting those who eat virtually no fruits or vegetables to eat the minimally recommended five servings daily could result in lowering the number of obese Canadians by 360,000. That would take a bite out of healthcare costs.

A second common concern with mandating more purchases from small farms relates to trade policy. Would such a mandate violate free trade agreements by placing imported food at a disadvantage? First, many American jurisdictions are also moving quickly in the direction of requiring sustainably grown food in their cafeterias. As the rules go, any country making a claim against another must first prove that it is playing by the rules itself. But more importantly the particular products that the government would require can, by nature, only be grown by small, nearby farmers.

GOVERNMENTS IN THE WRONG PARADIGM

In the fall of 2015, I met with Manitoba's then minister of agriculture. Walking up the steps of the Legislature, I couldn't help but think how much influence decisions made within that building have on the outside world. I was telling the minister about the successful first year of the Meechim social enterprise farm at Garden Hill First Nation. He was very pleased to hear the news. I then asked what his department did to support small farming operations. He and his deputy minister looked at each other and both replied, "nothing yet." The minister expressed surprise at how strong the small farm movement was and that it was emerging in all corners of the province. Yet his department was completely geared toward supporting big agricultural operations with crop insurance, risk management, and export-oriented incentives. There was nothing in the $200 million Department of Agriculture budget geared specifically toward Manitoba's small farmers. If we are to move to an age of problem solvers, this obviously must change.

MAKING IT EASIER FOR PROBLEM SOLVERS

There are many things governments can do to increase access to healthy foods in urban and rural areas in addition to procuring their food smartly in taxpayer-supported institutions. Some jurisdictions have

PLANTING THE FIRST TREE FOR THE MEECHIM FARM ORCHARD, IN GARDEN HILL.

Healthy Food Charters, which lay out plans that include, for example, planting orchards or gardens instead of shrubs and flowers (edible landscaping), using government buildings and parking lots for farmers' markets, and banning junk food from public establishments.

Governments need to ensure that prospective small farmers have the resources and information they need to enter the sector. Certification systems need to be accommodating to small operations to ensure food safety but at the same time easily enable small, new market entrants. Work can also be done to extend existing financial supports, such as crop insurance, to small operations. Governments could also support land trusts that would make land available to new entrants.

In her book, *The Economy of Cities,* Jane Jacobs writes that "Agriculture follows cities." Over history agriculture has developed not on its own accord, but it has been shaped by the demand for food in cities. What we eat determines what type of farms we have. If we want the food system to change, we must change our diets. Governments can play a role not by legislating what we eat, but by using their buying power and regulatory abilities to help shape a healthier society – one in which people have more good options and fewer bad ones.

Marketing boards and quota systems can also get in the way. For example, in Manitoba a farmer can't sell more than 1,000 chickens in a year unless she or he possesses a quota. Similar rules apply for potato and egg farmers. The quota system was designed to protect local producers from being pushed out of the market by cheap imports from large multi-national corporations, but it unintentionally restricts markets for small local farmers. The supply-management system may serve a useful purpose, but it needs to be amended to create additional space for small farmers.

Many small farmers also face legal obstacles. As one farmer pointed out, you can legally take your kids to McDonalds every day for greasy food, but it is illegal to sell eggs away from the farm. And for small farmers to legally sell jams or similar value-added products, they require inspected commercial kitchens.

Some governments also confuse what local food is all about. The government of Manitoba, for example, spent a lot of money to work with large retail grocery store chains to market "grown in Manitoba" produce. But because the chains needed large amounts of produce to fill their shelves, small producers were not able to benefit. In fact, all of this produce came from large farms that happened to be local. These stores sign year-long contracts for which most small farms cannot produce enough product. Even more troubling is the policy of the large chains to sign year-round fruit and vegetable contracts with country suppliers, making it impossible to buy Manitoba products even in season.

Regulatory systems, which are geared toward large players, need to readjust. Consider the example of Harbourside Farms, run by Clint and Pam Cavers in Southern Manitoba. They raise a variety of live-stock, run a small meat-cutting operation, and direct-market much of their meat. They are seasoned farmers and experts in the field of ar-tisanal sausage. In 2013, provincial officials raided their meat-cutting shop and confiscated thousands of dollars worth of speciality meat products over alleged food-safety concerns. The problem arose because there are no specific regulations applicable to their sort of operation. The regulations are geared toward operations like Maple Leaf, which processes up to 85,000 hogs per week in Brandon, Manitoba, not that far from the Cavers' farm. The irony is that just months before the raid on the Cavers' farm, they received an Award of Excellence from the Ministry of Agriculture for their meats. The minister himself tasted their (unknowingly contraband) products at the award ceremony.

THE DEFENCE OF BIG AG

I have long marvelled at the uniformity of the responses from people who make their living in the existing food system – some of them friends of mine – when confronted with the ecological harm, obesity, climate change impacts, and rural depopulation connected with the food sector. They all say the same thing: "We feed the world." They say that without the current system, more people in the world would starve because productivity would drop.

It is of course true, in the most basic sense, that farmers feed the world. The further claim that Big Ag is the only or best way to feed the world is more dubious.

First, farmers often grow what is profitable, not what feeds the most people. Think about corn for ethanol, barley for beer, and soybeans, which are used for a wide range of non-edible applications. Though a relatively small portion of Canadian crops go toward non-food uses, farmers need to be honest about whether they decide what to plant based on feeding people or making money.

Consider also that about three quarters of the grain grown in Canada is fed to livestock. Of course the livestock turn that grain into food – meat, dairy, and eggs – but the process is inefficient. Though different groups come out with very different numbers, it takes roughly six kilograms of grain to produce one kilogram of beef. If feeding the world is the bottom line, the whole food system should discourage meat consumption.

The assertion that high-input agriculture is the only way to feed the world is further undermined by the fact that somewhere between 30 and 50 percent of food grown in the world is wasted. This includes grain that spoils in large-scale storage facilities (especially in the global south), produce deemed too imperfect for sale, items that exceed their best-before date on store shelves, food still on the buffet spread at closing time, and the cheese going whitish in the back of your fridge. While it is too simplistic to think that the buffet leftovers would feed a starving child in Africa, the degree of waste points to food-system challenges more complex than just maximizing production.

Food spoilage is not a direct result of large farms, but it is a major social and economic issue that needs to be addressed. Steps are being taken in many jurisdictions to cut such waste through education about "best-before" dates and reduced prices on "imperfect" produce.

Another form of waste is overeating. Some experts say that overindulgence gobbles up enough calories to feed a billion people.

The experts in global food security and international aid have long stressed that world hunger is a matter not of food quantity but access. There is enough food in the world to feed everyone, but access in certain areas is limited for a variety of reasons.

YIELDS HIGHER?

Most importantly perhaps, the most comprehensive international study of agriculture simply did not support the view that large-scale, high-input agriculture is the best way to feed the world. The International Assessment of Agricultural Knowledge, Science and Technology for Development – a six-year, World Bank-initiated research project that involved 61 countries and more than 400 agricultural scientists – made the opposite finding. *Washington Post* columnist Barbara Damrosch summarized the report by saying that "small-scale, diverse, sustainable farms had the most potential to solve the world's hunger problems while reversing modern agriculture's devastation of our ecosystems."

My economics training taught me that larger production volumes of almost anything are more efficient than smaller ones. Economists call this "economies of scale." However I was intrigued to find out in my research that this may not be true when it comes to farming.

It turns out that economists have been debating whether there actually are economies of scale in agriculture. Emerging data supports an apparent "inverse relationship," meaning that productivity per unit of land goes down, rather than up, with increasing size. The debate is far from settled because there are so many variables, including soil quality, farming techniques, and weather. But the general point is that there is a legitimate debate, and it's not nearly as clear-cut as the Big Ag food-system proponents would have us believe.

Researchers at the University of California, Berkeley, recently published a comprehensive review in the papers of the Royal Society of London. After reviewing 115 studies on yields in 38 countries, they concluded that diverse organic farms already produce nearly as much food as conventional farms. Specifically, organic operations that rotate crops from year to year and employ "companion planting" (planting more than one crop, which enhances growth by providing nutrients naturally or allowing plants to protect each other from pests) have yields that are just 9 percent less than industrial methods. This relatively small gap is actually quite remarkable considering the billions of dollars in incentives, subsidies, and research that have been applied to increase yields in industrial farms over the last 50 years while support for the small farm model has been next to nil.

The researchers specifically mentioned "diverse" organic farms because alternating crops from year to year, as opposed to growing only a single crop, has consistently been shown to improve the yield of each crop by as much as 30 percent. Crop rotation tends to be more consistent and varied among small farmers.

GROWING OUR OWN FOOD

Small plots of land can also be brought into food production. The Forks, Winnipeg's largest tourist draw and a favourite hangout for the locals, has planted an orchard in space unsuitable for other uses. Some urbanists like to call this "edible landscaping." The Inn at the Forks also has a garden that saves them cutting their lawn and has the double benefit of providing fresh produce for their restaurant. Think of all the land that can be used for food production in your city without taking away from useable space.

And I wouldn't advise saying it can't be done, because it has been done. During both world wars, the Canadian Department of Agriculture launched campaigns with the aim of having "A Vegetable Garden for Every Home." Canadians used backyard spaces to plant vegetables for personal use and war effort. Expert gardeners were brought into the schools to get school children and their families interested in gardening. In addition to gardening, home owners kept hens for eggs and chickens for roasting.

And it wasn't just Canada that saw local food production grow exponentially. In the United States, the number of gardens reached 5 million during World War 1 and swelled to 18 million during World War 2.

Both my 85-year-old dad, who grew up in rural Ontario, and my 86-year-old father-in-law, who grew up in Winnipeg, remember working in their family's "victory gardens." The government slogan "Grow Your Own and Can Your Own" encouraged patriotism.

Just how much food can be grown in space that is currently yards? In Russia, after the collapse of the Soviet Union, a local food movement started. The impacts of the shift were chronicled by Dr. Leonid

Sharashkin and focused on the Vladimir region of Russia (published by University of Missouri in 2008). His work revealed that two out of every three households there are now growing over 90 percent of the country's potatoes and 80 percent of all vegetables. Also, 50 percent of meat and milk was also coming from micro producers. Now over 50 percent of food consumed (by value) in the Vladimir region is coming from household plots.

The bottom line is this: If the primary goal of our current food system were to feed as many people as possible, it would look entirely different than it does now. To defend the industrialized food system by simply saying "farmers feed the world" is simplistic. The current system is not designed to feed the maximum number of people, nor is it designed to produce the healthiest food, maximize environmental health, create good labour, or make rural communities thrive.

It's time for that to change. Again, this is not an affront to farmers; it is a call for creative collaboration between urban food advocates, people with access to agricultural land, and advocates of smart, efficient government. A healthier population and less volatile climate is in everyone's interest.

CHAPTER 7

CORRECTING THE CORRECTIONS SYSTEM

AN EMPLOYMENT SOLUTION TO AN EXPENSIVE CRIME PROBLEM

It was a curious place for a 32-year-old ex-gang member with a long, robbery-filled rap sheet. It was December 22, 2015, and Chris Courchene was roaming the aisles of a Winnipeg Walmart handing out money. The recipients were people who looked to him like they could use some help purchasing Christmas gifts for their children.

Chris's path to that Walmart was a long one. His mom, a residential school survivor, was a serious drug addict, so Chris grew up with his grandparents on the Sagkeeng First Nation, a two-hour drive north of Winnipeg. His grandparents were a positive influence in his life, and he did well there. That ended when his mother, living in Winnipeg, had him move in with her. Chris was old enough then to sell drugs to raise money to support her addictions.

I originally found this part of Chris's story particularly shocking – that his mother would have encouraged him to get involved in illegal activity. But it is not uncommon for young gang members to be pushed and pulled by family.

Aside from selling drugs, Chris committed a lot of robberies. He said that holding up convenience stores was his specialty. He'd often have an unloaded gun with him, as it made the process move along faster. Between the ages of 13 and 26, Chris was in and out of jails and courts. He thinks he was arrested more than 20 times. It could have been many more, but most of the time he didn't get caught for his hold-ups.

Every time Chris got out of jail, he would notice that his young cousins were taller. When Chris's son was born in 2007, he knew something had to change. Soon after, he was arrested for the last time.

"I was down on the ground face-first," Chris recounts, "with my hands cuffed behind my back and a police boot on my neck. I had had enough. I wasn't about to miss my son growing up."

A parole officer connected him to BUILD, a Winnipeg inner city social enterprise that hires people like Chris to do energy and water retrofits. Chris started working with BUILD in the summer of 2008. Since then he has received valuable on-the-job training and apprenticeship supports as well as parenting courses, help obtaining missing identification, a free bank account, a driver's license, and trades-based math tutoring. He has also attended workshops on financial management and budgeting. He has paid off driver's insurance penalties racked up in prior offenses, which included car theft. This is all part of the holistic approach BUILD takes when integrating people into the workforce.

Now Chris is a supervisor at Manitoba Green Retrofit (MGR) – a social enterprise that was set up to hire BUILD graduates like Chris. He is part of a team of 35 full and part-time workers who install high-efficiency furnaces, do apartment renovations, provide demolition services, and even do bedbug remediation. He also recruits for BUILD and MGR now, and if he signs you up, you can be assured there is significant peer pressure to live in a good way, to be conscientious about your work, and to be good to your family. Chris is a positive and strong mentor to other young men with difficult backgrounds who want to make something positive of their lives.

But how did he end up at Walmart with an open wallet? Amidst the memories of drug-induced violence and running from the police, Chris had hurtful memories of Christmases with his mom. "Your parents were supposed to look after you," says Chris, "and mine weren't able to. Christmas was no different than any other day for me except there was often more drinking."

Since being hired by BUILD, and then rising to the role of supervisor at Manitoba Green Retrofit, Chris and his partner Tammy have tried to make Christmas special for their two kids. This past year they were going to do everything right. It was going to be the perfect Christmas. He wanted more than anything for his kids to look back on their childhoods and know that their parents were there for them.

MGR SUPERVISOR CHRIS COURCHENE.

So Chris and Tammy saved up money for "really good" Christmas presents for their kids, and also for their nieces and nephews. They put a lot of thought into it, bought the gifts, and left them in the trunk of their car. Chris's plan was to put the kids to bed and, after they were sleeping, go get the presents, wrap them, and put them under the Christmas tree. When he went to get the presents, he discovered that his car had been broken into and the presents had been stolen.

Chris, who had been robbed before, recalled what life was like for him when he was the robber. "There's a code when you're running with gangs," says Chris. "You don't steal from kids." Chris knew firsthand what it was like to be an innocent victim of crime.

Chris made a plan. He would talk to his employer, MGR, and ask for a salary advance. He would pay it back after Christmas. He would pick up extra jobs on the weekends to make it all up. Disappointing the kids wasn't an option.

Lucas Stewart, the general manager at MGR, took the story to CBC radio, and this is where things really got interesting. Listeners donated money to help Chris get through Christmas. By December 22, his presents were replaced, wrapped, and under the tree. But he still had $1,500 left over, and he knew that this money wasn't for him.

While he had debts to pay and could have used the money, he set out for Walmart. Chris helped make Christmas a bit more special for the kids in 15 families. Many of the recipients burst into tears when they saw the scarred and tattooed Aboriginal man express his generosity.

BUILD CHANGED MY LIFE

I want to tell you how BUILD works, but first, let me tell you how I ended up there. In 2006, I was the Director of Energy Policy for the government of Manitoba. Natural gas prices had spiked and low-income families were having to choose between paying a utility bill and buying food. My co-workers and I had done some research on how other jurisdictions were responding. Some American cities had set up community-based non-profits that would organize trades professionals to insulate homes.

I phoned Tom Simms, an inner city community activist, and told him that Manitoba Hydro's Power Smart program wasn't reaching low-income families. I asked him if we could work together to set up an organization to do the insulating. Tom knew what the priorities of the community were. They needed jobs. So he said not to bother with the initiative unless inner city jobs were going to be created out of it.

Although we'd never heard of a social enterprise before, BUILD, the climate change and poverty fighter, was born. I began a very rewarding journey that day as well. I would soon leave government for a year to work at BUILD. I had every intention of going back to government, but I had unknowingly begun a career as a social enterprise developer.

I have to admit that, when BUILD was young, I thought guys like Chris were write-offs. I was wrong. For most of them, a job in a supportive environment arrests the criminal lifestyle dead in its tracks. This suggests to me that to fight crime and the costs associated with it, we should be creating jobs for this demographic. Social enterprises like BUILD have had tremendous success moving these inspiring men and women into the workforce. The problem is that, due to outdated government strategies, the people looking for work come to us in droves, but the training dollars and contracts come in dribbles.

MILLION-DOLLAR MEN

We call these chronic offenders the "million-dollar men" because that's easily the amount of taxpayer money we unnecessarily sink into many of them through policing, court, and incarceration expenses. According to Manitoba's Auditor General, since 2008 the provincial government has spent $182 million to increase prison capacity and will need to allocate another $600 million to meet projected demand. Add to this a $100 million annual increase in operating costs to provide staffing for the higher capacity, and it is safe to assume that, not including associated policing and court costs, a full $1.5 billion will be dedicated to this growing demand. In fact one of the former Manitoba NDP government's last acts before the April, 2016, election was to announce a new jail in Dauphin, Manitoba – a $40 million capital cost that they brazenly called a "healing centre."

PROFILE OF AN INMATE

Chris's story is surprisingly common. In Manitoba, 68 percent of the present and future occupants of these jails are Aboriginal. This is an astonishing figure given only 15 percent of our population is Aboriginal. These inmates often have substance abuse issues, no high school diploma, no driver's license, no work experience, and worst of all, no hope.

There is an even more alarming number. According to Statistics Canada, 75 percent of male inmates in Manitoba either reoffend or breach their parole conditions within two years of their release. Women getting out of jail have slightly higher re-offense rates due in part to complexities of the sex trade. We have come to call our jails "correctional institutions," as though they correct behaviour and somehow turn lives around, but with 75 percent re-offence rates, their report card shows a failing grade.

I've toured several of these "correctional institutions" and also work with people who have long histories with the correctional system. I can tell you there is shockingly little that happens in jails that gives inmates the tools they need to be successful upon their release. This is because governments think that restricting the freedom of people who offend will be enough to convince them to live productive lives. The stats do not support this.

If governments are really interested in reducing crime, they should start by looking at who is in jail and why.

Most inmates in Manitoba are Aboriginal, male, and repeat offenders. This is a common trend across the country but worse in provinces with high Aboriginal populations. This is not all they have in common:

- A 2008 Charity Intelligence report estimates that 80 percent don't have a high school diploma.

- The John Howard Society estimates that 55 percent have addiction issues and/or mental health issues.

• A 2008 study by Onashowewin cited that 88 percent or more of Aboriginal male inmates in Stony Mountain Penitentiary were in care when they were children.

• All front-line workers I have asked have estimated that 90 percent or more of the people they work with lack driver's licenses.

• 100 percent have employability issues such as criminal records, lack of experience, poor literacy, and no driver's license (front line estimates by several non-profits, including John Howard Society).

Given that most inmates are reoffenders, it seems painfully obvious that to curb crime and its associated justice, court, and policing costs, governments need to reduce reoffense rates by focusing on family reunification, drug treatment, mental health, education, and most certainly employment.

I have estimated in *BUILD Prosperity: Energizing Manitoba's Local Economy* that there are likely 25,000 Indigenous men in Manitoba with no access to the labour market. No matter how much they want to work, employment is out of reach due to barriers such as criminal records and a lack of grade 12 education, driver's license, and work experience. At the same time, there are 75,000 job vacancies expected in Manitoba in the next decade. So the easy question is: "Why don't these guys just go out and get a job?" The problem is that employers don't hire people who lack work experience, driver's licenses, and grade 12 education.

We need a plan to get these guys working. The good news is that it's entirely possible.

TWO PROBLEMS, ONE PROBLEM SOLVER

Part of the beauty of BUILD is that in addition to tackling high incarceration rates and costs, it also lowers utility bills. This work is important because many of Canada's low-income families live in older houses with inadequate insulation in attics, walls, and basements. While these houses may offer cheaper-than-average rent or require lower down payments than more efficient homes, their upkeep can negate the lower rent.

Just how much of a problem is high utility bills for low-income Canadians? Research by Green Communities Canada (GCC), a national
organization that supports community-based NGOs doing environmental work, documents the level of "energy poverty" across Canada.
In 2006 the average "energy burden" – the percentage of household income spent on utilities – of the highest income quintile was only 2 percent, compared to 7.3 percent for the lowest quintile. About one million
households spend more than 10 percent of their income on energy costs.

This figure is understated considerably because utility costs are often included in rent. "In other words", says GCC, "energy costs are often buried in rising rents, rather than showing up as increased energy
burden." And while one million households in Canada spend more
than 10 percent of their family income on energy, this doesn't include
water bills, which can also be high.

Within this context, BUILD started in 2006 with eight staff and
$300,000 from the Government of Manitoba. At the time, we hadn't
heard of a social enterprise. It hadn't occurred to us to do work *for* the
government (contracts for work in public housing). Rather, the model we
knew was to use government funding to fund the NGO to do the work.

In 2008 my colleague Lucas Stewart and I were driving past a
public-housing complex in Winnipeg and noticed several contracting
companies doing work there. I asked Lucas why Manitoba Housing
would hire them when we have long waiting lists of prospective employees and would do the same job for a similar price. He responded
by saying that they were contractors and we weren't. So on that day we
decided to become a contractor rather than just a non-profit program.
The beauty of it was that we didn't have to change much – just our
mindset. Manitoba Housing was happy too because it meant more income for social enterprises like BUILD who, in return, could hire their
tenants. Instead of relying solely on government funding, we could access trades-based contracts, which would help us greatly expand our
workforce. BUILD, the social enterprise, was born that day.

Over time we have expanded, though the basic model remains. In
total we have moved about 500 people into the workforce who otherwise would not have work. These 500 men and women, an army of

problem solvers unto themselves, have done energy and water retrofits at 15,000 Winnipeg homes where low-income people live, lowering utility bills by over $4 million every year.

In an average year, BUILD's revenues total about $2 million. Seventy percent is earned by completing contracts for insulating, water retrofits, and painting. The other 30 percent is funding from government, which is used for things like training, parenting courses, trades-based tutoring, and so forth. These costs are not normally incurred by contractors and so usually have to be covered by sources other than trades contracts.

BUILD trainees are motivated. One of our math tutors told me that one day a light went on for one of the students when he realized that, if he could get his grade 12 math, he could get into the apprenticeship system. And if he got into the apprenticeship system, his salary would nearly double. In this student's mind, his only barrier was figuring out how to calculate slopes, the measure of incline often used in construction. To laughter in the class, the student, a grade five dropout, picked the tutor up by his jacket collar and demanded that he teach him how to calculate slopes and wouldn't let him down until the tutor agreed.

BUILD's model has an impressive impact on incarceration rates. Without an intervention, 75 percent of people released from jail in Manitoba become involved with the justice system within two years of their release. At BUILD, this rate is just 20 percent. We have a steady stream of probation and parole officers bringing their clients to sign up for BUILD, as was the case with Chris Courchene. Unfortunately our waiting list of applicants is over four years long.

Not everyone's story is like Chris's, but many lives have been changed, and many families have been restored. Last year one of BUILD's trainees came to tell me he had just rented a five-bedroom house because he was getting his kids back from Child and Family Services. This type of story is not uncommon at BUILD.

These stories of changed lives have changed my own life. Though I now focus my work primarily on creating new social enterprises, I'm very grateful to continue my relationship with BUILD as a mentor. It continues to be a beacon of hope for many.

BUILD INC. STAFF ON A COMPLETED JOB SITE.

Since BUILD's inception we have mentored several other BUILD-like ventures that work in inner city settings. Manitoba Green Retrofit and BEEP (the Brandon Energy Efficiency Program) are both headquartered in Manitoba. Impact Construction operates in St. John's Newfoundland and Building Up is in Toronto. They all have important relationships with public housing providers, and most work at lowering utility bills. They hire people with little or no work experience, no education, no driver's license, and criminal records. We all have high stacks of resumes. But government response just doesn't meet the need. We find this frustrating because governments have every motivation to climb aboard.

Our costs are about $25,000 per trainee. Ten trainees cost $250,000 which is about the capital cost of just one jail bed or the operating cost to keep one person incarcerated for three years.

On average, each of the 500 people who have worked at BUILD have generated $80,000 in utility bill reductions over a decade, which are either enjoyed by low-income families or governments themselves. Governments are often the direct beneficiary because they are landlords or because they pay utility bills for social assistance recipients.

In 2013, the Canadian Centre for Policy Alternatives (CCPA) did a comprehensive study on the economic impact of governments and utilities investing in social enterprises like BUILD to do low-income energy-efficiency retrofits. The study used a common multiplier effect tool to determine the overall economic impact of the work. After applying the experience of BUILD, taking into account all costs, and comparing those costs with the value of all the benefits – including utility bill reductions, taxes being paid that otherwise would not be, saved incarceration costs, and reduced greenhouse gas emissions – the effect was estimated to be approximately 25.5 times the level of initial investment. In other words, for the $25,000 investment in training a BUILD participant, the overall benefit to the economy in reduced costs (reduced energy bills plus avoided jail, police, and court costs, social assistance, and so on) as well as benefits (taxes paid, work done, climate change benefits) is 25 times the $25,000. This effect is many times greater than a typical investment in a manufacturing plant.

BUILD and the other five social enterprises based on the BUILD model are not charities. They are not social services. They are not taking government handouts. They make significant contributions to shrinking government budgets, increasing the efficiency of the economy, and increasing the productivity of the workforce. We identify and eliminate waste: wasted energy, wasted water, wasted social spending, wasted tax dollars, and most importantly, wasted human potential.

NOW LET'S SCALE IT UP

In Manitoba alone there are 50,000 low-income households that, according to Manitoba Hydro, require energy-efficiency upgrades. There are roughly 25,000 Aboriginal men – and likely as many Aboriginal women – with no access to the labour market. And that's just one little province. The model works and the benefits are proven, so let's scale it way up. Let's do a million homes across the country.

Why isn't it getting done now? The problem, again, is that there is no policy framework to connect the problem solvers to the problem. Governments give out a bit of money here and there, but the overall policy understanding and the framework that could facilitate scaling up are lacking. Here's what it could look like. I'll provide examples of what provincial governments, municipalities, utilities, and regulatory oversight bodies can do.

FEDERAL AND PROVINCIAL OPTIONS

Governments can get far more bang for their buck by ensuring that social enterprises have first dibs on government contracts. This can be done by establishing procurement policies that give preference to social enterprises. This is a way for governments to use tax dollars to not only perform basic work – like installing low-flow toilets – but to ultimately reduce costs of social assistance, justice, and other social services.

In addition to linking social enterprises to these contracts, new markets can be created in public and private rental accommodations. In most rental units, tenants pay their own utility bills, so the landlord has little incentive to install a more efficient heating system or low-flow toilets since the savings would go to the tenants, not the landlord. The tenants have an incentive, but not the control, to make changes. To address this problem, governments can require landlords to meet basic, practical energy and water efficiency standards and make sure financing is available with retrofit supports that make replacement of inefficient boilers, furnaces, windows, and water fixtures fast and easy. The capital costs to do the work can be financed by utilities and paid for out of the utility bill reductions. Only work that has a good economic payback should be targeted. This is a win-win for tenants and landlords. Tenants get lower bills, and landlords get new heating equipment that is paid for out of the utility bill reductions, and not out of their capital budgets.

Just how great are the outcomes of this approach? For every 1,000 water retrofits in low-income housing, the utility bill reductions alone would reach $2.5 million over ten years.

REGULATORY BODIES

Provinces also control regulatory bodies that oversee energy and water utilities. Companies providing energy and water services to customers have to justify their rates before such bodies. Rather than focusing exclusively on rates, regulators should also be focused on lowering bills – especially for "hard-to-reach" customers such as low-income families and renters. Rate increases could be conditional upon meeting performance targets such as ensuring a percentage of low-income homes are insulated, with a significant percentage of this work to be completed by social enterprises each year.

MUNICIPALITIES

Most municipalities have water utilities. They could engage social enterprises to go door-to-door in low-income neighbourhoods and install water-efficient toilets and aerated showerheads for no upfront cost to the homeowner, landlord, or tenant. This can be paid for with temporary financing fees that would be much lower than the water reductions they would generate.

Because governments are operating within an old para
policy lever of choice to help homeowners do water retr

A SMART MUNICIPAL WATER BILL REDUCTION AND JOB CREATION PLAN BY THE NUMBERS	
COST FOR SOCIAL ENTERPRISE TO INSTALL AN EFFICIENT TOILET, AERATED SHOWERHEAD, AND FAUCET AERATORS	$400
TYPICAL ANNUAL WATER BILL REDUCTION FOR A FAMILY OF FOUR	$300 (THERE IS ALSO A REDUCTION IN HOT WATER USAGE THROUGH SHOWERHEADS AND FAUCETS WHICH WILL ADD $50 IN ENERGY SAVINGS)
MUNICIPALITIES COULD FINANCE THIS SERVICE BY APPLYING A $25 FINANCING FEE PER QUARTER FOR ONLY 16 QUARTERS.	$25X$16 = $400
SAMPLE QUARTERLY BILL BEFORE WATER RETROFIT	$375
SAMPLE QUARTERLY BILL AFTER RETROFIT ($375 MINUS $75 WATER SAVINGS PLUS $25 FINANCING FEE)	$325
WATER SAVINGS	30,000 LITRES PER YEAR PER HOME OR 300 MILLION LITRES PER YEAR OVER 10,000 HOMES
NET SAVINGS OVER A DECADE (NOT INCLUDING RATE INCREASES)	$1,000 PER HOUSE OR $10 MILLION ACROSS 10,000 HOMES
AMOUNT OF TAXPAYER DOLLARS WITH FINANCING APPROACH	$0

ally an expensive and administratively heavy rebate. Using the City of Winnipeg as an example, they offer $60 per home (in taxpayer money) to replace an inefficient toilet. I had a meeting with the official in charge of this program and asked him how effective the program was in low-income neighbourhoods. He went to check and found out, not to my surprise, that there was virtually no uptake in low-income ighbourhoods, where households are hardest hit by high water bills. ptake is low because low-income families generally rent. They are ith the bills that result from whatever appliances the landlord . And the landlord doesn't generally care about their utility bills because he or she doesn't pay the bills. So why would they bother spending money to replace toilets or inefficient furnaces?

If the City of Winnipeg changed its strategy to focus on low-income neighbourhoods by engaging social enterprises and implementing a smart financing strategy (paying for the retrofit out of the bill reductions), it would not only create jobs for people who need them most, it would save the cost of having to pay the rebates. It would also reduce administration and save low-income families hundreds of dollars per year.

An added benefit of water-saving programs for municipalities is that, in some cases, reducing water use can defer the need for expensive expansions of water-treatment capacity.

CROWN UTILITIES AND GOVERNMENT ENTITIES

All three levels of government own large entities like crown corporations. They fund new housing (through the Canadian Mortgage and Housing Corporation, for example), deliver health services (through hospitals and regional health authorities), provide energy and water services, and even, in some provinces, provide auto insurance. Governments can and should update the mandates of these entities to ensure that they are solving modern-day challenges. As Van Jones, the CNN commentator and American green jobs advocate says, "Match the people who most need the work with the work that most needs to be done."

In my home province, Manitoba Hydro's government-legislated mandate was written in 1960 when energy poverty and climate change weren't big issues. There is, for example, nothing in Hydro's mandate requiring them to lower utility bills for low-income customers. Nor is there any requirement to work with social enterprises. And any money they spend in this area must be justified at regulatory hearings, so they are naturally cautious and unambitious.

The new Progressive Conservative government in Manitoba has promised a separate efficiency utility. It will be interesting to see where this goes as their mandate unfolds. This dedicated efficiency utility w a main focus in my earlier book *BUILD Prosperity: Energizing M toba's Local Economy*. In my view, this idea has the most promis problem solvers to problems.

ARMSTRONG (PAST EXECUTIVE DIRECTOR OF BUILD INC.), AND WINNIPEG
US.

Each and every one of these government-controlled entities was established to solve a particular problem or to deliver a much-needed service. It only makes sense to modernize their mandates now to get the best value for their ratepayers and for taxpayers as a whole. Privately owned companies providing these same services can just as easily be mandated by law to meet society's present day needs.

NEXT LEVEL

Let's look at a three-point strategy to retrofit one million homes in Canada. Such a plan would create $5 billion in direct investment, save homeowners over $10 billion in energy bills over 20 years, create 78,000 direct jobs, and generate considerable indirect stimulus. Much of this work can be done by social enterprises. I've written about this strategy in detail which has been published by the CCPA.

First, focus on renters. Renters have been excluded from energy-efficiency programs to date because of the "split incentive" I discussed earlier. A tenant struggling with high utility bills is not in a position to retrofit a property that someone else owns. And the owner doesn't pay the bills, so he or she has no incentive to improve efficiency.

Interestingly, governments usually pay the utility bills for social assistance recipients, and since most social assistance recipients rent, social assistance budgets would see an impressive decline if the buildings in which welfare recipients live were to be retrofitted.

We need an aggressive strategy focused on renters to achieve these savings and ensure that social enterprises are trained up and ready to do a good chunk of the work. This can be done by simply requiring landlords to meet minimum energy and water efficiency standards and get social enterprises prepared to do the work. This strategy could save 400,000 renters $200 million annually in utility bills.

Second, zero in on reducing bills on First Nations. In most First Nations, more money is spent on energy costs than on housing. A national strategy to retrofit 100,000 First Nations homes would harne $500 million in retrofit work, save $50 million in annual utility ' and create 8,000 person years of First Nations employment. B the federal government will have to change its rules and r' that favour imported energy over home-grown renewable energy options that create local employment. Again, this money will circulate in the local economy rather than going towards importing energy from outside companies.

Third, target utility bills in low-income households. There are one million Canadian households that allocate 10 percent or more of their income towards paying their energy costs. Retrofitting half of these homes would increase disposable income for the families that need it most. This would have roughly the same impact as a permanent $500 annual tax-free subsidy. These 500,000 household retrofits would generate $2.5 billion in investment and cut annual utility bills by $250 million.

Problem solvers like social enterprises, insulation companies, and water-retrofit crews are ready and willing to create employment and cut utility bills. But it will only happen in dribbles until governments connect these problem solvers with the problems. We need minimum-efficiency standards for landlords, PAYS financing mechanisms available to First Nations across Canada, modern mandates for utilities, and regulatory rules that require private companies to lower utility bills for low-income families.

No government in Canada has yet decided to really embrace the work of social enterprises or the BUILD model, despite their proven track record of reducing crime, easing poverty, reducing government expenditures, and improving housing.

There are many more Chris Courchenes out there waiting to happen. Chris tells anyone who will listen that a job was what he needed to turn his life around. It's just too bad his mom didn't live to see her son succeed. She died of a drug overdose when Chris was in jail. Chris and I agree that she would be very proud.

CHAPTER 8

MAKING MONEY, MAKING CHANGE

SOCIAL ENTREPRENEURS

We have so far discussed social enterprises and the local food movement as problem solver examples. I would now like to add social entrepreneurs to that list.

Admittedly, the term "social entrepreneur" is broad. Social entrepreneurs can range from billionaires with scruples – think Elon Musk – to small-business owners who install solar panels. While they vary in what they do, they all have two things in common: They create markets for solutions to environmental or social problems, and they make money. They form an important part of the solutions economy.

The business sector learned long ago that there is nothing as powerful as a new idea in the hands of an entrepreneur. Social entrepreneurs find market solutions to both earn a profit and address social problems. They are usually individuals with innovative solutions to society's most pressing social problems. They are ambitious and persistent, tackling major social issues and offering new ideas for wide-scale change. They differ from social enterprises in that they are usually driven by the force of one person rather than a community. The most successful social entrepreneurs find what is not working and solve problems by changing the system, spreading the solution, and persuading entire societies to move in different directions.

The term "social entrepreneur" originated with William "Bill" Drayton. Bill was raised in Manhattan by parents who valued public service. The strong values of his upbringing blossomed in university. As an undergraduate at Harvard in the early 1960s, he invited prominent leaders from governments, unions, and churches to informal gatherings with students. The students could come and ask "how things really work." He called this the Ashoka Table, drawing on the na an Indian leader from the third century BCE who devoted his life to social welfare and economic development.

Drayton went on to study at Oxford, as a Rhodes Scholar, and at Yale Law School. Trained in economics, law, and management, he worked as a management consultant for most of a decade and then worked for the Environmental Protection Agency in the '70s, where he initiated emissions trading. He first used the term social entrepreneur in print in 1972.

Now Drayton serves as the CEO and founder of the largest network of social entrepreneurs in the world. Ashoka, which began with informal chats around the dinner table, is now an organization that includes 3,000 Ashoka Fellows in 84 countries. Ashoka provides support to its Fellows, who are creatively and successfully addressing stubborn social problems around the world. This book project is funded, in part, through Ashoka.

Ashoka Fellows are involved in everything from using rats to detect landmines in Angola to developing a scalable model for affordable dental care for low-income families in the United States to establishing an innovative model of childcare for women factory workers in Bangladesh. The organization is full of people who are brimming with creativity and caring.

Social entrepreneurs, whether connected to Ashoka or not, come in many different forms. I am particularly interested in those who use market forces for good. In some cases they identify waste and turn it into an opportunity. I think of my friends Rick Penner and Jennifer Peters.

SOLUTIONS EMERGE

Rick and Jennifer are both life partners and business partners. In 2001 they founded Emerge Knowledge, likely the largest recycling-software company of its kind in the world. Their service solution, called Re-TRAC Connect™, supports over 20,000 users across the world. The software makes it easy for recycling companies to track and analyze their data, report the amount of waste diverted, and share information their stakeholders. Their for-profit business helps governments the world by making recycling and waste management easier.

Before becoming social entrepreneurs, Jennifer had founded a successful employment-based non-profit helping social-assistance recipients gain access to the labour market, and Rick had a track record as a successful social enterprise developer. In 1991 he worked with a group of dedicated volunteers in Winnipeg to set up a store that sold donated, used building supplies and used the profits to support Habitat for Humanity, which provides housing for low-income families. With a name, a business plan, and materials that would have otherwise gone to the landfill, they opened the very first Habitat ReStore. Members of the public could buy used materials at very reasonable prices, support Habitat for Humanity, and divert entirely useful materials (hardwood flooring, used bricks, good windows) from the landfill. Today, over 900 ReStores across North America generate hundreds of millions of dollars in revenue.

EBERHARD AND MUSK

More prominent examples of social entrepreneurialism would include Martin Eberhard. Eberhard was born in California and received a master's degree in electrical engineering from the University of Illinois in 1983. He loved sports cars but also felt compelled to do something about climate change. The result was Tesla Motors, the stylish leader of the electric-car movement. Eberhard incorporated Tesla in 2003. Prominent billionaire Elon Musk joined the following year. Tesla's end goal is to see all cars on the road powered by electricity within the next few decades.

Musk, who founded PayPal, is a savvy businessman and a creative genius. He also cares about transformative change. Typical of social entrepreneurs who want to transform markets for good, in 2014 Tesla Motors announced it would share its technology patents with other car manufacturers in a bid to entice automobile manufacturers to speed up development of electric cars.

Musk also provided the initial concept, and financial capital, for SolarCity, the largest provider of rooftop solar energy in the Unite States. The underlying motivation for funding both SolarCity and la is to help combat global warming. Musk is also behind Tesla wall, a household-scale battery technology that could signif ter the electrical sector, opening new doors for intermittent renewable sources like wind and solar. Powerwall would affordably and efficiently take electricity generated from wind and solar when its available and store it in home-based batteries, ready to use when it is needed.

SOUS CHEF GONE WILD

Another social entrepreneur in a similar category is British celebrity chef and restauranteur Jamie Oliver. As a sous chef, Oliver was noticed quite by accident by a BBC film crew making a documentary. He went on to have his own cooking show and his celebrity status began to grow.

Oliver was not only a food celebrity, but also an entrepreneur. He opened a series of restaurants and sold a line of non-stick cookware. As Oliver's career unfolded, he became more of a social entrepreneur, using his businesses to get people eating healthier food. In addition some of his restaurants in London have begun to work with disadvantaged young adults who wish to have careers in the restaurant business.

In 2005 Oliver initiated a campaign, originally called Feed Me Better, to move British schoolchildren towards eating healthy foods and cutting out junk food. As a result the British government also pledged to address the issue. His emphasis on cooking fresh, nutritious food continued as he created *Jamie's Ministry of Food*, a television series in which Oliver travelled to inspire everyday people to cook healthy meals.

Oliver saw an opportunity to improve his company's value, and also to sell more healthy food, when he was approached by Sobeys, Canada's second-largest food retailer. Sobeys has grown to reach $20 billion in annual food sales at their 1,300 retail outlets. In the summer of 2013, Sobeys launched a new slogan and marketing strategy, which they called "Better Food For All." Jamie Oliver's objectives of increasing healthy eating and Sobeys' objectives of increasing their profits came into alignment. Sobeys would use Oliver's endorsement to promote their sales of healthy food. In exchange Oliver would talk to their customers through their advertising and encourage them to eat better ʲ. It's entirely possible that Oliver's intervention in Canada's food ⁻y has had more impact in encouraging families to eat healthy n most government healthy-eating advertising campaigns.

Eberhard, Musk, and Oliver have each used their stature and business acumen to both encourage and meet demand for products that address social issues, while also making a profit.

HOW TO SAVE OLD GROWTH FORESTS

Another similar example is Ashoka Fellow Nicole Rycroft. During a 1993 four-week blockade of the Clayoquot Sound old growth forest on the coast of British Columbia, she came to a realization: "It was just a matter of time before the logging trucks made it past us and the magnificent cedar trees we had been protecting would be gone. I knew there had to be a better way." She recognized that it was the economy that was creating demand for old-growth forest trees and that it must be possible to change the economy. She went on to found a company called Canopy.

Canopy works with the forest industry's largest customers to protect the world's forests, species, and climate. Her first big success was convincing the Canadian publisher of the Harry Potter series to go green, and from there the entire Harry Potter book series internationally followed suit. She would meet with business executives and turn them into champions of conservation and sustainability. Canopy has already transformed the purchasing practices of 750 of the forest industry's largest customers – from book publishers and printers to leading clothing brands and fashion designers – to create permanent and practical solutions for the world's threatened forests. Canopy's brand partners include H&M, Sprint, Penguin Random House, Levi Strauss & Co., Stella McCartney, The Globe and Mail, and Guardian Media Group.

EVERYONE A CHANGEMAKER

Ashoka supports successful social entrepreneurs around the world. But they also believe that everyone has a bit of heroism in them. The organization's mission has evolved to include a focus on enabling an "everyone a changemaker" world. According to its website, "Ashoka believes that anyone can learn and apply the critical skills of empathy, team work, leadership, and changemaking to be successful in the modern world." Through its recently launched Ashoka Changemaker Sch
and Ashoka Campuses, the organization seeks to equip people

cially young people, with "the skillset and a connection to purpose so that they can contribute ideas and effectively solve problems at whatever scale is needed in their family, community, city, workplace, field, industry, country."

I am excited about social entrepreneurialism in all its varied forms. The bottom line is to think creatively about problems, pushing beyond the charity model – though there is certainly a place for that form of compassion – and pushing past merely articulating problems to reach the nitty-gritty work of proposing and enacting innovative solutions.

To quote Bill Drayton, "Social entrepreneurs are not content just to give a fish or teach how to fish. They will not rest until they have revolutionized the fishing industry."

CHAPTER 9

MEASURING CHANGE
A 'SEVEN GENERATIONS' ECONOMY

I could hear the drums and singing coming from inside the Portage Place mall in downtown Winnipeg as I approached. It was January of 2013, and I was on my way to join an Idle No More rally. There were so many people that the friendship round dance enveloped the entire mall. Everyone felt welcome to participate. Security guards and police stood by knowing that, due to the sheer size of the crowd, they would be helpless if the group had any nefarious ideas. But in the spirit of the Idle No More movement, the event was peaceful and respectful. All of us who were there felt hopeful for the days to come, not only that Indigenous people in Canada would someday be able to participate fully in the economy, but that traditional Indigenous values would be core to decision making in Canada and around the world.

As I have at other Aboriginal ceremonies and events, I had a strong sense, as I listened to speakers at the mall rally, of the difference between traditional Aboriginal values and the values that guide the prevailing economic mindset. Speakers at these events talk about the importance of accessing clean water, of taking care of the earth, and of making sure all families, not just Indigenous ones, have the tools they need to be successful. It is a very community-minded perspective. And that community extends into the future.

The most important difference, in my view, is that our current system is based on short-term thinking while Indigenous philosophy is based on a long-term perspective. Elders from many Indigenous traditions teach that we must consider the impacts our decisions have on people who will live seven generations from now. What we do today should ensure that people seven generations from now can flourish.

John Ralston Saul, a leading public thinker, sees profound value this worldview. In his 2014 book, *The Comeback*, he responds to cerns that some Canadians have regarding a small number of A

nal people gaining control of large tracks of land through the Treaty
Land Entitlement processes.

> *The question we should be asking is quite different. . . . Why
> don't we want [land] controlled by Canadians who feel strongly
> that this is their land? By people who want to live there and
> want their children and grandchildren to live there? Surely
> they are the people most likely to do a good long-term job at
> managing the land.*

Ralston Saul goes on to question the short-sightedness of the Euro-
centric approach to the economy:

> *The only other option we have is for the government to hand
> control of the land to a dozen directors of a corporation sitting
> in Toronto or New York with no long-term interest. They simply
> want to extract the minerals or timber, extract the wealth from
> the land, and move on.*

What would a "seven generations" lens bring to government decision making? Leaders today struggle with forecasts of sluggish economic growth. For a hundred years we have relied upon growth in our
economy to provide the funds necessary to pay for public investments
in education, healthcare, and infrastructure. This growth has fueled
the increase in our standard of living. But what happens now that governments are forecasting very low growth rates and therefore very limited growth in government revenues? How do governments respond
to societal needs for more comprehensive healthcare, better education,
and affordable housing? How do they address climate change?

The stagnation in the global economy is so alarming that Japan recently announced negative interest rates – that is to say that their central banks are actually paying people to borrow money in hopes that this
will spur spending, investment, and therefore growth in the economy.

But the seven generations outlook, as I understand it, offers a com-
ﾟetely different perspective on this crisis. This alternative outlook is
ﾟly encouraging.

MEASURING PROGRESS

Building jails, cleaning up oil spills, consuming fossil fuels, and treating diabetes all have one thing in common – they contribute positively to Gross Domestic Product (GDP). Because they are creating economic activity, they are deemed to be good for the economy. The GDP is a measure of the value of goods and services that a country produces. It is the chief economic indicator used around the world. Bankers, bond traders, voters, governments, and the media all work from the assumption that the higher the GDP, the better.

But GDP is a narrow and nearsighted way of measuring the performance of an economy or country. Any economic activity is chalked up as good, regardless of negative social or environmental consequences. Paul Hawken – an American entrepreneur, environmentalist, and author – once said, "We are stealing from the future, selling it to the present, and calling it Gross Domestic Product."

The short-sightedness of GDP-based decision making over the past several decades is causing our poor economic results. GDP does not distinguish between a dollar spent putting someone behind bars and putting that same person to work. It does not distinguish between a dollar spent on crappy food and a dollar spent on healthy food or money spent to treat disease versus money spent to keep people out of the healthcare system. It likes a dollar spent to destroy the environment just as much as a dollar spent to ensure a strong environmental future. Our fundamental way of measuring our economy is steering us blindly toward problems instead of solutions. It cares about the money that is flowing now, not healthy people, families, and ecosystems for generations to come.

Of course there are alternatives to the GDP – alternatives that are more in keeping with a multi-generational outlook and more in keeping with a social enterprise outlook. One such tool is the Genuine Progress Indicator (GPI). Rather than just measuring the value of goods and services produced, it also takes into account environmental and social factors. The GPI increases with high employment rates, high family income, more parks, more leisure time, more libraries, and so on. The GPI decreases when things like crime, pollution, green gas emissions, deforestation, and unemployment increase. It has a much better capacity to ensure that the economic activity now does not undermine the well-being of people and the planet in the future.

Within the GDP mindset, governments simply look for ways to stimulate growth. Within the framework of the GPI, the question is more one of what we can do within our economy to increase our well-being. Put simply, it is a call to repurpose billions of dollars in current expenditures towards investments that will increase the overall welfare of people and the planet both now and into the future. As discussed in previous chapters, this would include diverting money spent on incarceration toward social enterprises and treatment of offenders. It would include using food-system subsidies to invest in the small farm movement. It would focus health expenditures on healthy living, not just treatment. And it would redirect fossil fuel-sector subsidies toward energy-efficiency projects and renewables.

If we want an economy that values problem solving, an economy that meets people's needs, we must value economic activity that produces desired outcomes and devalue economic activity that detracts from social and environmental goals. We need more good growth and less bad growth. We need an economy that considers the impact it will have seven generations from now.

CHAPTER 10

ON UBER AND COMPLEMENTARY CURRENCIES

MODERN TOOLS FOR OLD PROBLEMS

Approximately 1.6 billion people in the world have no access to electricity. Many of them rely on kerosene, charcoal, or diesel for lighting or cooking. These options are not only expensive, they also cause poor indoor air quality and, because they are fossil fuels, create greenhouse gas emissions.

In the old paradigm, dominated by big government and/or big business, the approach to meet this electricity demand would be to build large power-generation projects by damming up rivers or mining coal. Those who identified themselves as being on the left side of the political spectrum would want a government agency to own and operate the generating station. They would also want to ensure that the project would go through environmental licensing processes, that the costs be regulated by an independent agency, and that the workers be represented by unions who would ensure fair treatment. Those on the right would want the project privately financed with as little regulation as possible. They would argue that the free market should determine who benefits and who doesn't. They would want to charge a maximum price for the power. Regardless of which path were followed, the approaches are very top-down, and there would be both significant upfront costs and significant environmental degradation.

The new paradigm, however, offers a very different path forward. The approach would be to focus on problem solvers. These ventures are usually small and medium-sized, and they operate in the best interest of the communities in which they operate. They ensure that the environment is well protected.

SIMPLE COST-EFFECTIVE SOLUTIONS

So what to do about the 1.6 billion people with no electricity? Enter a charitable company called M-KOPA, which has installed solar at more than 375,000 homes in Kenya, Tanzania, and Uganda. For just $75, families receive a small 8-watt solar panel and battery pack. The system is enough to power three lights, charge up to five mobile phones, and power a radio. The customer pays $25 up front and pays the other $50 in daily payments of 13 cents through their mobile phones. They own the system outright in just one year. The great thing about the deal is that each family saves an average of $750 per year using the solar system instead of buying kerosene. M-KOPA is so successful that over 2,500 people in these three countries alone are employed to convert over 550 new homes each and every day.

Kiva is another example of a simple but transformative way of backing problem solvers. The San Francisco company offers no-interest, no-fee loans to "entrepreneurs who are doing amazing things." As of July, 2016, Kiva has loaned $874 million to 1.5 million small-scale entrepreneurs in 83 countries around the world. Many of these entrepreneurs are sustainable farmers, others offer renewable energy solutions. Over 75 percent of the entrepreneurs receiving Kiva loans are women. One young mom of five children lives in a refugee camp in the West Bank and raises goats to sell the milk and meat. Another 22-year-old mom in Zimbabwe empowers local girls in her community by hiring them to make and sell homemade juice and healthy snacks.

Kiva's costs of connecting the lenders to the borrowers are covered by donations, so the loans can remain interest free. Some of the organization's work involves evaluating each entrepreneur. Most loans start out small, but as dependability is demonstrated, loans can become larger. Over $2.5 million is loaned out each week. Kiva also gives those of us with money to invest the ability to be a part of the solution. Over 1.5 million lenders from all over the world choose which venture they wish to support by contributing as little as $25. Once the original loan is paid, the contributor is invited to reinvest the money, making it a growing and growing fund. Over 97 percent of the loans are paid back.

IPHONES TO THE RESCUE

Like M-KOPA, Kiva's approach is dependent on creative financing with loans that are usually paid back through mobile phones. But these less developed countries aren't the only areas of the world taking advantage of light-weight solutions. We are also seeing this economy emerging in our backyards here in North America.

Uber is the now well-known, San Francisco-based ride-sharing service. The model works because it helps solve traffic woes not by making wider roads, but by putting riders into empty seats – or in other words it is a technology-based solution that connects available resources (empty seats) with demonstrated needs (people who need rides). Ride seekers use an app on their smart phone to send a trip request. Uber drivers can accept this trip request and provide the ride in their own cars. No money is exchanged during the ride. The riders pay Uber, and Uber pays the driver. Both drivers and riders get rated based on their behaviour, which encourages politeness. According to Wikipedia, as of May, 2016, the service is available in over 66 countries and 449 cities worldwide.

Airbnb uses a similar concept. It is a service that connects people who need a temporary place to stay with homes that have unused beds. Founded in 2008, it already has over 1.5 million listings in 34,000 cities and 190 countries.

COMPLEMENTARY CURRENCIES

As I continued to hear of Uber's growing popularity and the success of ventures such as M-KOPA and Kiva, I wanted to explore what, if any, benefits this approach would have for solving poverty and environmental problems in Canada's low-income neighbourhoods. It turns out that combining smart phones with creative financing would be a great way to empower problem solvers right here at home.

My friend Wadood Ibrahim is the co-founder of a Winnipeg-based, employee-owned company called Protegra. We discussed the problem of money being used in ways that don't benefit the community and what can be done about that. Wadood is ideally suited to discuss subject because Protegra recently launched "The Local Frequen an innovative app-based rewards program exclusively for locally-owned and independent businesses. Users must first download a free app, then make their purchases from participating businesses using either cash or debit. Each purchase earns the customer 3 percent back in "Local Points." These points can then be spent at any Local Frequency participating business. There is no cost to using the app because the 3 percent fee that usually goes to credit card companies such as MasterCard, Visa, or American Express is instead converted to a local currency.

Local currencies, also called complementary currencies (as they function alongside federal dollars), are issued by an entity other than a government or central bank. Just like Canadian Tire can issue its own "currency," so can small communities or community organizations. These currencies are generally intended to support the values and aspirations of a community. This is an important feature because money in low-income communities tends to leak out. Complementary currencies can ensure that money circulates to support rebuilding the local economy. Complementary currencies are primarily designed to encourage spending in a specific geographic area or to be used for a specific purpose, such as purchasing healthy food.

One of my favourite examples of a complementary currency is in the Brazilian city of Curitiba. Under the visionary leadership of mayor Jamie Lerner – a legendary problem solver – the city offered residents of *favelas* (shantytowns) bus tokens in exchange for delivering bags of garbage to drop-off points. This is yet another example of using available resources, in this case empty bus seats, with real needs, like promoting garbage collection. This approach was important because there was no well of money to pay for a new fleet of garbage trucks, and the garbage trucks couldn't navigate the streets in the *favelas* anyway due to narrow streets. Offering bus tokens as a de facto form of currency worked well because busses were often not full anyway, so the cost to the city was not particularly high. Plus, bus tokens were often of particular value to *favela* residents in that the tokens allowed them better access to the labour market.

Carrot Rewards is a very different example of a complementary currency. A $7 million pilot project of Health Canada and the BC govern-

ment, the program gives Aeroplan and Petro Canada points to partici-
pants who are eating healthy, walking a thousand paces more than their
daily average, and taking health-related quizzes on their smart phones.
Essentially it is a wellness app. The idea has caught the attention of
both the Canadian Diabetes Association and the Heart and Stroke
Foundation, who are partners in the project.

Somewhat similarly, the Ontario Power Authority recently offered
homeowners Air Miles if they improved the insulation in their homes.
This was after its mass advertising strategy around home insulation
yielded low participation rates. The reward program resulted in a five-
fold increase in participation at half the cost of the advertising approach.

GARDEN HILL BUCKS

So what would happen if we threw together smart phones and a complementary currency in a place like Garden Hill First Nation? I'll use that
example because it is a project some of us are working on right now, but of
course it could be adapted to suit any situation where there are problems.

First, every adult in the community would be supplied with a smart
phone. This seems like a steep upfront expense, but when governments
realize the cost-saving advantages of this approach, one would hope
that they would be quick to come on board.

Second, we would need a local currency. For now, let's call it "Garden Hill Bucks." A community like Garden Hill is a perfect place to
implement a complementary currency because so much money is now
going towards undesirable outcomes via purchases at the Northern
Store – an outside-owned company whose overall healthy food sales
are miniscule. The store also, for a stiff fee, cashes cheques, as there is
no other financial institution in the community. These factors mean
that much of the money in the community immediately leaks out of
the local economy rather than circulating.

Garden Hill Bucks could be spent at Meechim Foods where only healthy food is sold. The bucks would be accumulated and tracked on smart phones and could be received for various things, including:

- Eating healthy, exercising, and watching videos (in English or Oji-Cree) on health-related topics. (Health Canada should be very interested in investing because they would know their dollars would go directly towards lowering their future expenditures significantly).

- Bringing garbage and recyclables to a central drop-off point. (Indigenous and Northern Affairs Canada currently has enormous liability due to a lack of proper garbage pick-up and disposal and a lack of electronics and hazardous waste recycling; this lack of service is causing toxic runoff into local land and water).

- Increasing democratic participation in local decision making by attending community meetings, voting, filling out community surveys, and volunteering at community events.

- Exchanging inefficient light bulbs and inefficient shower heads for more efficient alternatives.

- Having children use apps that promote Indigenous language learning and retention.

- Loading social assistance cheques directly onto the phones in Canadian currency, thus bypassing the current cheque-cashing bottleneck and fee structure at the Northern Store.

This list is just a potential start. Many more possibilities exist.

There are many examples of good government intentions not getting desired results. One is the million or so dollars per year in Nutrition North Canada subsidies going to a store that sells only a small amount of healthy food relative to its overall sales. Another is the $35 monthly social assistance increase for people with diabetes on First Na-. These two things together, and other efforts, are clearly not doing the trick. The prevalence of diabetes, and the costs associated with it, is increasing rather than decreasing. Wouldn't it make more sense for the $35 to be given in Garden Hill Bucks so they would certainly be spent on healthy food? If, as we discussed earlier, governments were to estimate their future expenditures in areas like diabetes, they would quickly bump up the $35 to something much more significant, knowing that all of it would be spent on healthy food.

Initially, Garden Hill Bucks would be redeemable at the Meechim local healthy food market. As time goes on, more local eligible retailers would pop up because bucks would be circulating in the economy rather than leaking right out.

In addition to these benefits, a good local smart phone network could be used to inform people of community events, weather warnings, safety alerts, police notifications, community business updates such as Band Council Resolutions, job postings, training opportunities, and specials at the local Meechim healthy food market.

The possibilities are nearly endless. A group of people at Garden Hill could be trained to look after the currency and the smart phone usage. Only community-building actions should be allowed and there would need to be an approval process regarding what messages get sent out and when.

This form of integrated problem solving could prove to be a highly affordable way for governments and low-income communities to achieve desired outcomes. Investment in such solutions may soon become very attractive.

Problems have solutions. But these solutions may not be the ones we're used to.

THE
REINVENTION
OF
GOVERNMENT

CHAPTER 11

REINVENTING GOVERNMENT

A WORD TO BUREAUCRATS AND POLITICIANS

When I knock on government doors, I am quickly reminded that it's a rough world for problem solvers. Rather than being embraced and encouraged, we tend to be treated like problems. When citizens come to government officials with cost-cutting, creative proposals to solve expensive problems, they should be welcomed with open arms. They should not be met with words like, "we can't afford to do that," or, "it would set a dangerous precedent."

Most people would agree that more job training for ex-inmates would significantly reduce incarceration and related costs, but there is very little money for the cause. Most people would agree that eating more fruits and veggies would reduce health costs, but support for better food policy is limited. Most people would agree that it doesn't make sense for governments to subsidize a cucumber flown into a remote Indigenous community but not a locally grown cucumber, and yet Ottawa just expanded that exact subsidy program. Most people would agree that social assistance is not a dignified or sustainable solution, but more and more is spent on welfare cheques every year.

What gives?

POVERTY HAS NO CAUSES: DEBUNKING FALSE NOTIONS

Over and over again, I have come across three falsehoods about poverty. It is these false beliefs that lead to governments designing healthy food programs that leave out local food production or that confine decisions to focus on problems rather than problem solvers. Let's briefly look at these three falsehoods.

The first falsehood is that there isn't any money. In fact, there is lots of money. But too often it is spent on problems rather than solutions.

Governments pour more and more money into treating diet-related diseases such as diabetes while subsidizing and supporting a food system that offers a lot of bad choices. As I discussed earlier, in Manitoba the provincial government is the single largest buyer of food – for hospitals, prisons, and other institutions – yet it does not use that purchasing power to create a healthier system.

Governments in many places spend huge amounts on policing, courts, and incarceration instead of investing in employment and rehabilitation programs, which are proven to be a much cheaper way to address public safety and recidivism.

Governments subsidize phosphorus-intense agricultural practices while trying to address nutrient loading in water bodies such as Lake Winnipeg.

Put simply, the problem is not a lack of money but poor use of it.

The second falsehood is that low income people don't want to work. Within the social enterprise community that I'm a part of, we are inundated with job applications from low-income people. Some social enterprises have waiting lists more than four years long. Some don't advertise job vacancies because they don't want to get people's hopes up. I've helped interview 57 people for 15 entry level geothermal jobs. I've reviewed 112 resumes for six temporary demolition jobs. I've gone through a stack of 100 resumes of people who wanted to work on a First Nation farm.

I see people who don't know how to work, or don't have the skills to work, or have barriers preventing their entry into the labour market – such as low literacy, disabilities, lack of child care or housing, or addictions – but it's rare to see anyone who really doesn't want to work.

Against my better judgement, I agreed to speak at an inner city job fair a few years ago in Winnipeg. In my presentation, I outlined to the job seekers present that our social enterprises hire people with little or no experience in the labour market, with criminal records, and with no driver's licenses. The response was electric. It wasn't long before security guards were called to help me get out of the room as desper-

'.L FOR 8 LABOUR POSITIONS AT 7 AM IN WINNIPEG'S NORTH END.

moms and dads were shoving resumes aggressively at me. I was so very sad that we were not able to hire them all.

The third falsehood is that poverty has causes. This was addressed by Jane Jacobs, the American-Canadian journalist, author, and activist best known for her now widely accepted theory that cities should consist of relatively densely populated, interesting neighbourhoods rather than sprawling suburbs. Jacobs was also a noted economic theorist. In her 1969 book, *The Economy of Cities*, she wrote that "poverty has no causes." When poverty activists hear this, they are usually perturbed, as I was when I first read it. It goes against everything we have been told about poverty.

So if poverty has no causes, how is one to address it? Jacobs observed that poverty is nothing more than the absence of prosperity, and if we want to reduce poverty, we should be promoting prosperity. Here's how she states it:

> To seek 'causes' of poverty . . . is an intellectual dead end because poverty has no causes. Only prosperity has causes. Analogically, heat is a result of active processes; it has causes. But cold is not the result of any process; it is only the absence of heat. Just so, the great cold of poverty and economic stagnation is merely the absence of economic development. It can be overcome only if the relevant economic processes are in motion.

Instead of focusing only on treating the symptoms of poverty, which can be very costly, Jacobs argues that we must promote prosperity. Grand Chief Sheila North Wilson uses the example of driver licensing in her preface to this book. A look at job postings will confirm that about 75 percent of vacancies require a driver's license, yet I would estimate that more than three quarters of adults who are chronically unemployed don't have a license. A large portion of unemployed people are immediately disqualified from a large portion of available jobs. A better solution is to give people the tools to be prosperous – give them access to community-based driver's training. If governments were really concerned with reducing poverty, we would have easy-to-access community-based driver's training programs right across the country. Out of our modest surpluses, BUILD offers a driver's training program. But it should be available to everyone to significantly improve their employability.

Many anti-poverty activists argue for higher social assistance rates on First Nations. While I'm not entirely opposed to that, wouldn't it make more sense to supplement social assistance by offering families a "good food box" that is filled with chicken, fruits, and vegetables raised and grown by a local social enterprise? What about an aggressive strategy to employ people to install geothermal and solar? What about building a social enterprise centre in every First Nation to be a hub for economic activity as has been done in Winnipeg's North End?

So yes, we need a whole suite of solutions to help people prosper. This includes literacy, affordable housing, addictions treatment, child care, and parenting supports. But to understand poverty, we must see it in a new way. Problem solving is not about masking the symptoms of poverty. It is about giving people and communities the tools they need to be successful.

CONNECTING PROBLEM SOLVERS TO PROBLEMS

All over the world, there is a new paradigm emerging in which small-scale economic agents are creatively solving social and environmental problems. How do we go about making the "ecosystems" that will quickly usher in a new problem-solving era?

The institution of government, at least as we currently know it, is in trouble. Sluggish growth rates, constrained budgets, and growing debt are the norm. Real solutions for social and environmental problems are nowhere on the current horizon. The dollar amounts required to refurbish and expand infrastructure are larger than anyone who is in power dares mention. Billions are spent on more and more police officers and jail beds that don't offer meaningful solutions, and health budgets perennially push governments to the limit despite decades of efforts to control spending. It gets tiring to hear of the same approaches to the same problems over and over again.

It almost seems like governments have stopped believing that problems can actually be solved. That's because they are focused on the problems rather than the problem solvers. Incarceration doesn't make an employment problem go away. Cleaning up diesel spills in remote First Nations doesn't prevent more diesel spills. Subsidizing a monopoly, profit-driven retailer to sell healthy food will not change the incidence of diet-induced diseases. But the solutions economy sees the opportunities behind the problems.

Here are five ways governments can create space for problem solvers, or in other words, how they can create markets for solutions.

NEW MANDATES FOR INSTITUTIONS AND NEW REGULATORY FRAMEWORKS

Most of our existing regulatory regimes, crown corporations, and even legislative frameworks were designed to meet the needs of society decades ago. Current challenges are different. Most of this government architecture has not been updated and continues on as though we live in a different era.

One good example of this is in my home province of Manitoba where our sole energy utility has a mandate that was written in 1960. It is no surprise that, on average, it hooks up 25 new homes a day to the natural gas system – here in a province with abundant job-creating renewable-energy options. And regulatory rules focus on achieving low energy *rates* with very little focus on *low bills* – which is especially important for hard to reach low-income customers. In Manitoba we ask the same utility to increase its sales and at the same time to encourage its customers to be "Power Smart."

Outdated mandates are commonplace all across the country. The Canada Mortgage and Housing Corporation has no money for First Nations social enterprises to install geothermal systems at time of construction. Rather, it favours high-cost, imported energy. The Freshwater Fish Marketing Corporation won't allow local fishers to sell their catches locally. Indigenous and Northern Affairs Canada, which administers social assistance on First Nations, will pay any and all utility bills but won't pay for systemic changes that have rapid paybacks and create local employment.

Most government programs are focused on funding one-off projects rather than transformative and systemic approaches. The federal government's ecoENERGY program will subsidize high-cost, low-impact projects, such as a solar panel on a single building on a single First Nation here and there, rather than community-wide, low-cost, high-impact approaches.

I come back to the Van Jones quote I used earlier: "Our defining issue is connecting the people who most need the work with the work that most needs to be done." Our first task in getting there is making sure our institutions, government mandates, and regulatory frameworks are up for this task.

BARRIER REMOVAL PROCESS

Governments should set up transparent and accountable processes to invite stakeholders to report barriers that prevent problem solvers from being successful. Cabinet ministers, or their empowered designates, should be made aware of these barriers and have them removed in a timely fashion. Each department should have a champion that can quickly and efficiently remove barriers that prevent the re-emergence of the local economy.

For example, government healthy-food incentives exclude job-creating, local food approaches, and non-profit social enterprises are usually ineligible for small-business support programs. Ministers and civil servants seem to agree that these rules need to be changed, but there is no process to change them. No one seems to have the authority to make these changes, as commonsense as they may seem.

PROGRESSIVE PROCUREMENT

Currently government procurement strategies are geared to awarding large contracts to large companies. There are two issues with this approach.

First, it passes up an opportunity to use government purchasing power to increase the capacity of the problem solving sector and ultimately get far more bang for the taxpayer buck.

For example, social enterprises can complete contracts for public and non-profit housing providers. They hire people to paint, landscape, roof, insulate, do water retrofits, replace inefficient furnaces, install windows, and clean apartments. The more work they can acquire,

STAFF OF MANITOBA GREEN RETROFIT.

the more people they will hire who may not otherwise have access to the labour market. Social enterprises can't provide all the goods and services that governments need, but the more social enterprises grow, the happier taxpayers will be in the long run.

Second, governments need to think outside the box about what they're procuring in the first place. Do they want diesel hauled in to remote communities at the cheapest rates, or do they want heat and electricity sourced locally from renewable options in a fashion that creates local employment and business opportunities? Because if they want the latter, procuring diesel fuel won't achieve that outcome. Do they want to focus on what rates people pay for energy and water in public and non-profit housing, or do they want to decrease bills through, for example, low-flow water fixtures and high-efficiency furnaces?

Some public institutions are already changing the way they procure. Manitoba Housing is a national leader in engaging social enterprises that, in turn, hire their tenants. Diversity Foods, as we discussed in Chapter 6, is another excellent example of value for dollar. Imagine the boost to the solutions economy if all taxpayer-supported institutions across Canada got on board.

END PERVERSE SUBSIDIES

Governments choose to spend money on a range of subsidies that contribute to problems. These dollars need to be reallocated towards problem-solving ventures, though in the form of forward-looking investments, not simple subsidies. The obvious example is support for the fossil fuel industry instead of renewable-energy options. But there are other examples as well. Should governments continue supporting monopoly grocery retailers on First Nations instead of supporting social enterprises that sell only healthy food so that they may transform local economies?

EXTEND THE PAY-AS-YOU-SAVE MODEL

Governments need a mechanism to enable them to invest in problem solvers now though the savings will only come later. There needs to be a way to bring the future savings forward to the present so that smart money can be spent now on solutions, rather than later on problems. The Manitoba social enterprise community lobbied hard for a system called Pay-As-You-Save (PAYS) to help us lower bills in low-income housing. I described earlier how this works. What has become very evident to me however is that this model can also be used in other areas to lower costs.

It is this PAYS mechanism that has allowed Aki Energy and its partners to install $6 million worth of geothermal systems on First Nations in just three years. There is no way we could have completed this much work, let alone the $100 million worth that we expect to do in the next decade, relying solely on federal funding. Water, energy, and even cable companies have used this approach for over 100 years to reach their customers. Utilities install water, sewer, electrical, and natural gas infrastructure then get their investment back over time through charges that are imbedded into their rate structures. Why not use it for renewable energy and energy-efficiency options?

Simply put, PAYS puts money up front for measures that are guaranteed to pay for themselves over time. The utility gets the upfront financing back through the guaranteed utility-bill reductions. The financing is attached to the building and not to the people living there – it's not a loan. This makes dollars available to everyone easily. If you move the benefits stay with the house and the financing fee stays too. This is a creative way of bringing the benefits forward to the present day to allow for investment.

At the moment, PAYS is only widely available in Manitoba and only for customers of Manitoba Hydro. The federal government can connect problems to problem solvers by making this tool available across Canada for installing renewable-energy and energy-efficiency infrastructure.

This proven model can be applied much more broadly than just the energy sector. Governments can offer to finance any and all ideas from reputable non-profits that can deliver real savings to taxpayers. This could apply to programs that reduce incarceration and recidivism rates or it could apply to preventative-healthcare measures. Governments would provide funding up front and collect their investments back over time with associated reduction in departmental budgets. Actual

INNOVATING OUR WAY OUT
OF THE CHILD WELFARE CRISIS

There are 10,000 children in care in Manitoba alone and 8,900 of these are Aboriginal. Everyone agrees that current approaches aren't working to prevent this outrageous human tragedy. Something must be done. It must be innovative, transformative, family centred, and cost effective.

The child welfare system is not structured in the best interest of at-risk children, youth, and families because the approach is focused on keeping the children "safe" from their parents by apprehending the children rather than working with the parents to keep the family together and safe.

In the Family Drug and Alcohol Court of the UK, its founder, Judge Nicholas Crichton states that, "some parents demonstrate a remarkable capacity to change in response to our more constructive, empathic approach." Keeping families together minimizes the impact of change for not only the parents, but also for the children and youth.

There has been a move in the last decade to devolve the management and operation of child welfare agencies to First Nations. While there are aspects of this that are helpful, few people would consider Indigenous child welfare to be Aboriginal people apprehending Aboriginal children. Indigenous child welfare is focused on keeping families together.

INDIGENOUS CHILD WELFARE
CENTRES ON KEEPING FAMILIES TOGETHER

The good news is that there are many good examples re-emerging that are showing promise. These approaches are working but are reaching far too few families due to lack of funding.

Some examples include Nisichawayasihk Cree Nation and Misipawistik First Nation, which are responding to crises by removing the parents from the home rather than the children. Then, subject to available funds, they circle the parents with the supports they need to be healthy and good parents.

Ma Mawi Wi Chi Itata offers its Family Group Conferencing (FGC) program in Winnipeg, When an Aboriginal teen becomes pregnant, they involve members of the child's extended family and support network.

Together they work to come up with a plan to support the parents, and if the parents aren't in a position to support the child, they try to keep the child with relatives. The families of both the mother and the father are invited to participate, and organizers say the turnout is usually good. The program is filled with success stories, but funding is needed to expand it to reach more families – and keep more kids out of care.

With PAYS, Ma Mawi Wi Chi Itata could put together a costed expansion proposal and include evidence of direct savings to the government. If the government is in general agreement with the benefits and costs, and has confidence in the service provider, the proposal would be financed (not funded). The Department of Family Services would then pay back the upfront costs out of the savings that result from the intervention. In most cases the costs are a small fraction of the direct savings to government. Again, as with the Pay-As-You-Save model used in the energy-efficiency sector, the Department of Finance would provide the resources up front, and the Department of Family Services would pay the "financing fee," which would be paid for out of their reduced expenditures caused by having fewer children in care.

The FGC is a prime example of the new paradigm. The current system has government intervening from the outside rather than working with family and community from the inside out. The government is looking at risk avoidance by apprehending children rather than looking at a risk sharing model in which broader family units are engaged. The FGC is also a very Indigenous approach in that it's not just the immediate family unit that is involved – rather the more broadly defined family unit. Instead of government looking at their expenditures as costs, FGC provides government a very affordable way to resource families.

In Manitoba the main push in child welfare was, for a decade, the creation of a cabinet committee made up of eight cabinet ministers all responsible for programs that had something to do with children. This is a response from an old paradigm in which governments are expected to solve problems. Governments are not going to solve the child welfare crisis, but community innovation will – and governments must ensure the conditions exist to allow these problem solvers to emerge.

savings must be closely monitored to help make decisions about expanding the activity or moving on to other ideas.

In the case of a measure that reduces incarceration rates (and expenses), the Department of Finance would provide the financing, and the Department of Justice would pay the "financing fee" out of its savings. Savings should not include reductions in existing workforces or wages but would focus on alternative approaches that are not currently being done. So rather than procuring the cheapest way to build or staff a jail, the PAYS approach would focus on alternatives to the jail in the first place.

CAN GOVERNMENT AFFORD PAY-AS-YOU-SAVE?

Can cash-strapped governments afford to front money for PAYS-style initiatives? The short answer is that the more money that is invested in the PAYS system, the better. Whether money were to go toward, for example, keeping children out of care or lowering government-paid utility bills, the more financing (offered only in cases with a high probability of ultimately saving governments money), the better. It would lead to a dramatic increase in creativity and a decrease in the need for government programs.

SOLUTIONS QUOTIENT

Just what quantity of resources should be put towards solutions? How can governments prioritize growing the impact of the solutions sector? As a senior civil servant with the Government of Manitoba, I had experience with the Treasury Board process within government. Every dollar is scrutinized with a focus on *how* the money is spent. Are there receipts, was the expenditure approved, and so on. There is next to no analysis of, or thought given to, the *impacts* of the support on future spending. For example building sprawl now means more fire halls, more schools, more busses, more police stations, more snow removal, and more maintenance later. Similarly, there is no comparison of, for example, a million dollars spent on a new jail and a million dollars spent on training that cut recidivism rates by two-thirds. Much of this can be addressed with independent cost-benefit analyses but the system needs a jolt to make sure resources are available for solutions.

Government needs real fiscal discipline. A practical way forward would be to estimate additional future expenditure requirements in high-growth spending areas such as incarceration, policing, diabetes treatment, and so on and then dedicate 25 percent of what's going to be required to solutions. It's entirely possible that much of the new money for addressing problems won't even be needed because of the investment in problem solving. I would propose we call this budgetary methodology is "The Solutions Quotient."

The level of public trust in governments is generally low. Many people do not trust their elected officials or civil servants to make good use of their tax dollars. Social enterprise solutions could help restore some trust and thus revitalize democracy. Governments need to place greater trust in the social enterprise developers and in the sorts of people social enterprises hire. In turn, as results accumulate, perhaps the public would place greater trust in government. A focus on smart government could replace the tired arguments about the size of government.

SOCIAL IMPACT BONDS

Some jurisdictions have proposed social impact bonds (SIBs). This is a variation of what I've proposed above, except that the private sector provides the financing instead of the government. If done properly this is better than the status quo of doing nothing, but there are several unavoidable problems. The first is that the private sector will require a healthy rate of return meaning that some or all of the savings would go back to the entity providing the financing rather than back to taxpayers. (An alternative to this would be to invest public pension money). The second issue is that the financier could cherry-pick the most profitable ventures. They might focus on men in the incarceration system, for example, rather than both men and women or urban centres rather than rural or northern centres. Due to the involvement of the private sector providing the financing there needs to be checks and balances put in place with independent verification. This process can have the unintended consequence of making government larger than it need be. These issues present challenges in terms of meeting the full range of public needs in a way that best serves the taxpayer and society.

WHY ARE GOVERNMENTS NOT JUMPING
ON THE SOLUTIONS BANDWAGON?

Like me, you might be wondering why in the world it is hard to get governments to embrace practices that help them solve problems and save money. What exactly stands in the way?

Based on conversations with others who have worked in senior roles in government, let me suggest the following factors. First, there is an inertia of established programming. Civil servants are not only familiar with established programming; their job descriptions are tied to it. Politicians and the public are also familiar with the way things are. Change takes mental and organizational effort. It is easier not to change.

Second, lobbying interests tend to focus on levels of funding for existing programs, and decision makers too often get caught up in the pressure from these different interests instead of stepping back from those misdirected debates. They should look long and hard at what actually works and what doesn't, not just how much money goes where. The current process leans very much toward a managerial mindset rather than a transformational one.

Third, governments tend not to trust non-profits. They feel that funding non-profits will result in a loss of control over the expenditure of taxpayer dollars. More non-profit support means more liabilities. More liabilities mean more oversight. More oversight means more bureaucracy. Of course evidence-based, measurable outcomes would deal with this concern.

Lastly, governments like to avoid risk. In the example we used in Chapter 5, Aki Energy's transformative financing model was blocked by the federal government. Why? Because INAC was not in control. Transformative models, by their very definition means communities don't need permission of a civil servant to move forward. The obvious concern here is that they will make poor decisions leaving INAC holding the bag. The solution to this is to work on solutions together. INAC can be at the table, say on the board of a social enterprise. This way the risk can be mitigated (rather than avoided) and what risk there is can be shared.

THE FUTURE OF PHILANTHROPY IS
SOCIAL ENTERPRISE

Along with his brother Craig, Marc Kielburger founded the successful
charity Free the Children. Mark and I were recently speaking at an
event in Toronto about change making. He said that their charity
started out by building schools in impoverished African communities
and that, while they are proud of that, they more recently started
a social enterprise called "Me to We," which is transforming entire
communities by changing their economies. "Me to We" provides
good incomes to community members by buying merchandise
made in these communities and selling it around the world. He
stated that the "future of philanthropy is social enterprise."

In addition to the revenues that flow back to artisans and
manufacturers in poverty-impacted communities, there have been
$17 million in profits since 2009. These profits are split evenly
between reinvestment in the social enterprise and their charity,
Free the Children. This concept isn't all that new because non-
profits like Oxfam and Mennonite Central Committee have been
buying and selling fair trade items for decades. What is new is that
mainstream charities are starting to get on board and in a big way.

One of the reasons charities are innovating is that the demands
on their services are ever increasing, but access to new dollars
is limited. This should sound all too familiar because the
same is true of governments. Just as charities are focusing
on changing economies, so too should governments.

AN OPEN INVITATION FOR INNOVATION

Governments must facilitate and encourage the emergence of the solutions economy. If they did, we would see that the community sector can provide services with much better results than the status quo.

This approach would blur the lines between the public and community sectors and get real and measurable positive outcomes for everyone involved, including taxpayers and citizens in general. Making it easier for problem solvers will reward good ideas, setting in motion an unstoppable force of community-minded, entrepreneurial innovation.

CHAPTER 12

THE END OF WELFARE

THE CASE FOR A COST-NEUTRAL BASIC INCOME GUARANTEE

Up to this point, I have focused largely on tools that problem solvers need. In this chapter and the next I will briefly turn my attention to two essential tools that people need to be successful. I'll start with a Basic Income Guarantee, sometimes calls a Guaranteed Annual Income or Citizen's Wage.

How does this fit with social enterprises and the solutions economy? The promise of the solutions economy lies partly in its ability to convert waste to opportunity, and this includes the waste generated by the current social-assistance model.

In order to get people working, and using government services less, we must talk about welfare – not reforming it but replacing it with something fundamentally different.

The idea of a Basic Income Guarantee (BIG) keeps popping up in the news. Quebec Premier Philippe Couillard has set up a cabinet committee, saying he's "dead serious" about implementation of a BIG. The committee is headed by Labour Minister, François Blais, who has written a book on the subject.

Elsewhere in the country, the Ontario government has announced BIG pilot projects, and federal Minister of Families, Children and Social Development, Jean-Yves Duclos, has expressed interest in making a move as well. A BIG is also being considered by several cities in the Netherlands, including Utrecht, which will begin a pilot in 2016. Finland is also moving to set up a BIG for some of its citizens.

DOES WELFARE WORK?

Why all the interest now? The short answer is that social safety nets are not working. Financially stressed governments can't afford them, and recipients are inadequately served. The even shorter answer is that welfare is a bad idea. As I stood in Garden Hill watching people collect their cheques, I was not observing a phenomenon that is fundamentally good. The solution is not higher welfare rates but something entirely different.

Some people are unable to work, often due to a disability, and they need a dignified means to continue living a meaningful life. Welfare, or social assistance as it is now called, does not provide enough for a dignified life, and there are usually humiliating processes to go through to be considered eligible in the first place.

For those who are able to work but cannot find employment, welfare provides a meagre existence, and it confronts people with what is known as the "welfare wall." People trying to get off social assistance by working part time or generating some income in other ways are penalized, as new income is clawed backed. There is a built-in disincentive to work.

A friend of mine is on disability due to a health problem. She found her social assistance benefits very difficult to live on. To help address the situation, she planted a garden. A social assistance worker was checking up on her and noticed on her Facebook account that my friend had a garden and her monthly check was reduced significantly as a result.

At best the process is cumbersome and stressful. At worst it is humiliating and dysfunctional.

Social assistance is also expensive, in part because it is an administratively intensive program. One reason Dutch politicians are considering a BIG pilot project is that an estimated 20 percent of their social assistance budgets get gobbled up by the bureaucracy.

Most provinces struggle to contain their social assistance budgets by making eligibility criteria more stringent and keeping benefits low. This adds further stress to the system and can result in people falling through the cracks.

The social safety net is stretched, ineffective and tangled. It need not be so.

WHAT IS A BASIC INCOME GUARANTEE?

The BIG is not a simple replacement for social assistance. It is fundamentally different than simply raising social assistance rates. Here's how it works. It replaces the full range of income support programs for low-income households – including social assistance, child tax benefits, GST rebates and others – and uses the income tax system to replace those supports with a simple across-the-board income top up for everyone below a "guaranteed" level. That level would be higher than current social assistance rates, allowing individuals and families a more dignified and less stressful existence.

Otherwise known as a "negative income tax," the BIG ensures an acceptable family income by using the income tax system to top up income to a minimum floor. Part of the strength of the BIG is its simplicity. It cuts out a lot of bureaucracy, achieving significant savings. There is no need for intricate criteria, reviews of every application, and the like. And of course there is no need for the various income-support programs now in place. This would serve everyone in a dignified fashion. No one would fall through the cracks.

The other big selling point is that, as pilot projects and studies demonstrate, an investment in higher incomes for people who need it results in health and justice savings. If people facing a difficult phase of life are given dignity, stability, and a reasonable income, they will be less likely to require healthcare services, including mental health services, and they will be less likely to get in trouble with the law, whether because of gang activity, domestic abuse, or something else. Individuals and families will be less likely to need to move, which can cause extra stress especially when kids need to switch schools.

Given that 93 percent of Manitoba inmates are male and 68 percent are Aboriginal, a good way to find out how a BIG would impact the justice department budget is to ask at-risk Aboriginal men. I sat down with a dozen of my coworkers at BUILD, the Winnipeg-based social enterprise that hires many ex-offenders. The group wholeheartedly agreed that having an income each month would have kept most of them away from gang activity. A BIG would significantly reduce the number of people selling drugs or committing robberies. As informal as this survey was, the result is welcome news as all levels of government need to reduce ballooning justice and policing budgets.

The savings from cancelled programs, such as social assistance, along with significantly reduced administration costs are what make the BIG cost-neutral for governments. The level of the BIG, which would vary from region to region, would be calibrated according to expected savings.

Detractors generally think that the BIG would cost money. This is why I advocate for a cost-neutral approach to start with (some people advocate for higher levels). Just take the savings and design a system that would use that amount. This can be done to ensure that no one is worse off and a whole lot of people are better off. It's hard to imagine anyone disagreeing. More efficient, more humane, and cost-neutral. Sure, we'd still have poverty, but there'd be a lot less of it.

Five BIG field experiments were conducted in North America in the 1970s. The outcomes were remarkably consistent. The most extensive of these studies was conducted in Dauphin, Manitoba. Thanks to recent work by professor Evelyn Forget of the University of Manitoba, new conclusions are now being drawn, including that the BIG caused an 8.5 percent drop in hospitalization. There were fewer mental health issues, fewer domestic-abuse issues, and even fewer work-related injuries (likely caused by less home stress brought into the work place).

WON'T PEOPLE JUST STAY HOME AND WATCH TV?

The biggest knock against the BIG is the belief that many adults would choose to stay home and live off the BIG rather than work. The field studies do not support this, except in the cases of parents staying home longer after the birth of a child and young adults choosing to finish high school or other schooling before entering the labour market. Both of these would have positive effects on society and the economy.

My experience has shown me over and over that people want to work. The exceptions are much rarer than some people's stereotyped perceptions. The BIG represents a different attitude toward people. It places greater trust in them. It does not humiliate them; it does not kick them when they are down; it does not watch over them like a parent. Because of this I believe it is less likely to create a sense of dependence. It is also more flexible in terms of allowing people to ease back into the labour market without fearing repercussions. For instance under the existing system a person on disability might not dare attempt to see what work they are able to do for fear of program administrators cutting them off altogether with claims that they are not actually disabled at all.

Advocates for the BIG come from across the political spectrum. One of the first and most important proponents of the BIG was Milton Friedman, a fiscal conservative legend and former advisor to US Republican president Ronald Reagan. Conservative Canadian former Senator Hugh Segal proposed that the federal government implement the BIG across Canada, leaving the provinces to redistribute the savings to other priorities.

Medicare started in Saskatchewan, and when the benefits were shown there, it was adopted across the country by the federal government. The Canadian government should implement a large BIG pilot either in Quebec, Ontario, or Manitoba. The first two provinces have shown interest, and Manitoba is the place where much of the BIG-related research is centered. Governments at all levels have to work together because the benefits are at all levels. It wouldn't make sense to have a BIG offered at the federal level with, for example, provincial social assistance still in place.

One of the hallmarks of the solutions economy must be that governments begin to focus on problem solvers and move away from creating problems. Governments need to meet the needs of their citizens, encouraging productive work and doing so in an affordable manner. Moving from the traditional social safety net to a Basic Income Guarantee would be an important step in this direction.

CHAPTER 13

A $15 PER HOUR MINIMUM WAGE

FULL-TIME WORK SHOULD PAY THE BILLS

"We either need more affordable housing or more people that can afford housing, or both." That's what Lawrence Poirier, general manager of Kinew Housing, says. Kinew Housing is one of the largest non-profit providers of housing for Aboriginal families in Manitoba. In his 30-plus years working at Kinew, Lawrence has seen the demand for affordable housing increase significantly but the ability to pay decrease. Housing costs and wage scales are out of alignment for too many Canadians.

The same is true south of the border where governments are taking concrete steps to address the gap between wages and the cost of living. California and New York State both decided this year to raise their minimum wages to $15 over the course of several years. Various cities have taken similar measures. In other jurisdictions specific sectors have secured similar gains. Low-wage employers like Walmart and McDonalds have announced more modest wage increases in response to the mounting pressure. Some of that pressure has come from media reports showing that some "McEmployers" pay such low wages that their own full-time workers and their families need to rely on government assistance and charity to help them get by. While there is certainly push-back to the $15 wage, momentum in favour of significantly higher wages is clearly building.

In my home province of Manitoba, nearly 40,000 people earn the minimum wage of $11 per hour. The number is closer to 100,000 people if you include those paid $12 or less. Some people imagine minimum-wage earners as teenagers working part-time to earn extra spending money. In fact 80 percent of minimum-wage earners in Manitoba are over the age of 20. Sixty percent are women, 58 percent are full-time, and about half work for corporations with over 500 employees. So this isn't just teenagers flipping burgers.

THE COST OF FINANCIAL STRESS

A low minimum wage is not enough for a stable, healthy, dignified life. It is a recipe for household stress. It means that people have to strain and stretch and worry. In many cases it means parents have to take a second job (or third) instead of spending time with their kids.

To fill the gap, governments spend roughly $1.5 billion annually in Manitoba on social assistance, tax credits, tuition grants, and income supplements, much of which is targeted at the working poor. If low-income workers earned more, the need for government subsidies would decrease.

A good example is the former Manitoba NDP Government's December, 2015, announcement of $22 million in annual rent assistance for low-income earners who spend more than 25 percent of their annual income on rent. For a single parent with two kids, working full-time at minimum wage, the program, called Rent Assist, would provide $742 per month in additional income. If, over their 17 years in office, the NDP had raised the minimum wage to $15, the result for the parent would have been about the same, but without the government expenditure.

The mayors of both Calgary and Edmonton have expressed support for Alberta Premier Rachel Notley's commitment to bump the minimum wage up to $15 over her mandate in part because this will reduce the need for income-related supports offered by their city administrations. In other words, they understand that a $15 per hour minimum wage actually decreases the size of government. Arguing against the increase is an argument for bigger government.

IS A HIGH MINIMUM WAGE A JOB KILLER?

Of course some people argue that increasing the minimum wage would backfire by forcing companies to lay off employees. Critics say high minimum wages kill jobs and hurt our competitiveness. They say the jobs will go to China. These criticisms deserve attention. First, today's minimum-wage earners are not generally in the manufacturing sector, so the argument about China is a stretch. China cannot wait on your table at a restaurant. The fact that minimum-wage earners are not in the manufacturing sector also largely negates the argument about our competitiveness in the international market.

As for higher wages killing jobs, the research does not support this claim. Putting money in the hands of low-income people is a good way of getting more money flowing in the economy. And minimum-wage earners spend a good portion of their income on the sorts of businesses that employ people at the bottom end of the wage scale. Consumer spending is the major factor that drives job growth in that part of the economy.

In a recent comprehensive study on the impacts of significantly increasing the minimum wage, David Green of the Institute for Fiscal Studies in London, England, concluded that claims of "massive job losses [due to minimum-wage hikes] in low-wage sectors of the economy are just not credible." In a separate study released in 2014, economists Jordan Brennan and Jim Stanford looked at 30 years of Canadian minimum-wage data and found no evidence that minimum-wage levels affected employment either positively or negatively. While there may be some job losses, these are offset by new hires in sectors where consumer spending fuels growth.

The Canadian Federation of Independent Business responded with a study that asked their members whether they would be more or less likely to lay off workers if their labour costs went up. Of course the response was negative toward minimum-wage increases, but such a question is flawed. They should have also had their members consider whether if their sales also increased – due to the impact of the rise in disposable income – they would be more or less likely to hire more workers.

POLICY SOLUTIONS
Like the Basic Income Guarantee, a $15 minimum wage is an integral part of the solutions economy. There is a whole segment of society that is struggling. The creative and productive capacities of these people are largely wasted. Their children are put at a big disadvantage. At the same time, they end up over-utilizing government support programs. It's a double whammy of unmet potential and high costs to government.

The BIG, $15 minimum wage, and solutions sector are largely about turning these struggling people into thriving citizens, to the benefit of everyone.

This is a bold goal, and it requires bold action. The solutions economy is part of a new paradigm, and you can't get to a new paradigm incrementally. Here in Manitoba, the former NDP government instituted tiny minimum-wage increases in each of their 17 years in power, but because the increments were so small, they only got it up to $11 an hour. Their lack of enthusiasm for a high minimum wage came out during their last, losing election campaign in 2016, during which they promised to continue with small increases so that, if they were re-elected, the minimum wage would be only $13 an hour by 2021. They were replaced by the Progressive Conservatives, whose first budget contained no increase to the minimum wage.

A transformation is taking place with respect to minimum wage. Workers are fed up, and more and more policy-makers are understanding that trapping people in near-poverty does not create a healthy society or economy.

If we want an economy that solves problems, we need to raise income for the working poor. It's time for real change. And to the working poor, real change starts at $15 an hour.

CHAPTER 14

AGREE TO AGREE
TRANSFORMING THE POLITICAL SPECTRUM

Bruce Carson had completed one crack deal and was on his way to another when he dropped off his resume at BUILD. Bruce had heard about BUILD from a friend and thought it might give him a chance despite him having no driver's license, a long police record, no experience in the formal labour market, and no grade 12 diploma. When I first met Bruce, he was typical of the type of workers BUILD would hire: low in confidence, lacking hope, and beat up from being incarcerated or in the child welfare system.

Many governments would treat Bruce as someone to fear. Fear is potent political capital. He would have been the justification for more police, tougher laws, and bigger prisons. He would have been the reason to vote for the toughest-sounding party. That was the old way of seeing things. But the conventional paradigms are changing.

About 30 years ago, many southern Republican-run states set about to reduce their public-safety problem by increasing incarceration rates. Republican Jerry Madden of the Texas House of Representatives said recently that the policy of mass incarceration in Texas seemed like a good idea at the time. Texas, like other states, hired more police officers, lawyers, judges, and correctional officers. And they built more jails. At one time they had one out of every 20 citizens behind bars.

Over time two problems became evident. First, crime rates went up instead of down. Sixty percent of ex-offenders were reoffending within 11 months of being released. The second problem was the cost, which ballooned by 600 percent. Leaders in Texas have slowly admitted that the experiment failed. It failed the people who entered the prison system, and it doubly failed the public who were stuck with the bill and didn't have a safer society.

WHERE ARE CANADIAN CONSERVATIVES WHEN WE NEED THEM?

The high-profile American conservative group, Right on Crime, says American conservatives believe in "cost effectiveness," and they aren't finding it in the justice system. Republican stalwarts like Texas Governor Rick Perry, former Florida Governor Jeb Bush and former House Speaker Newt Gingrich support an alternative to the "tough on crime" policies that were, for a long time, the political orthodoxy for both Republicans and Democrats. They, and many others, have signed on to the Right on Crime statement of principles, which says that "Criminal law should . . . [not] be wielded to grow government and undermine economic freedom." They say the "tough on crime" approach delivers "diminishing returns" in the cases of non-violent offenders. The sharply conservative group advocates for "reforming offenders."

They say that, "by reducing excessive sentence lengths and holding non-violent offenders accountable through prison alternatives, public safety can often be achieved consistent with a legitimate, but more limited, role for government." On one hand it sounds odd to hear hardline conservatives departing from the decades-old party line. On the other hand, it makes a lot of sense.

The other odd thing is that Canadian politicians of all stripes seem to have missed the lesson. Here in Manitoba our former NDP government supported Stephen Harper's old school tough-on-crime agenda. Rather than defending taxpayers or applying lessons from the US, our Justice Minister said his government "was prepared to meet the cost" of the provincial portion of the federal government's strategy to increase incarceration. The Canadian Parliamentary Budget Officer issued a preliminary estimate that the total cost of the Conservative "crackdown on crime" would be $2 to $3 billion, and about three quarters of the incarceration costs would fall to provinces.

Despite this there was no defence of the taxpayer from the Canadian right. Nothing from the business community or so-called taxpayer groups. Is sitting idle in an expensive jail cell a conservative value?

While the current federal government is not pursuing the same sort of minimum-sentencing, zero-tolerance policies as the previous government, it has not articulated a bold vision for change. It still lags well behind many American Republicans.

WHAT DOES IT MEAN TO BE A CONSERVATIVE?

There are many kinds of conservatives. Most of them agree that government should be small. Big government, they say, just slows down the private sector and saps taxpayers. Many conservatives say that welfare discourages people from working, high taxes discourage companies from investing, and social programs get in the way of people being successful. The less government, the more freedom. The more freedom, the better off we all are.

Sometimes the strengths of conservative values get lost in their own narratives. I was recently a guest on a national right-wing radio talk show. One of the callers challenged my view that it makes sense to employ ex-inmates so that their chances of reoffending decline. He saw this as preferential treatment, and to him that was completely wrong. I asked him what made more sense – spending $220,000 to build a new jail cell to house an unproductive occupant or offering employment options that would have that person working and paying taxes?

Another example of conflicted conservatism is the traditional view on minimum wage. As I pointed out in the previous chapter, a low minimum wage contributes to higher government spending on support programs for the working poor. But if full-time workers had more money, they wouldn't need to stand in line at food banks or receive taxpayer-funded supports.

Ironically, in this case, government that gets out of the way of the market by not setting higher minimum wages leads to bigger government. A low minimum wage also contravenes the conservative value of rewarding hard work. Similarly, increasing the role of government to address causes of criminal behaviour can lead to smaller government. In both cases the productive capacity of the workforce increases, as does the efficiency of government.

David Frum, the Canadian-born, American Republican icon, has been musing publicly about how his party needs to reform. In a CBC radio interview, he quoted former British Prime Minister Lord Salisbury, who said, "there is no error of politics more deadly than sticking to carcasses of dead policies." Frum argues that the Republican economic platform of lower marginal tax rates for the wealthy and deregulation of government were seen by Americans to have grown the economy but that these policies will no longer work. He says conservatives need new policies for a new set of circumstances.

While Frum has not spoken about the solutions economy, it would not be hard to imagine someone like him seeing the sense of governments creating space for social enterprises, as they are fiscally responsible, entrepreneurial, increase the productivity of the labour force, and result in more affordable government.

Social conservatives who are beginning to campaign for progressive social issues are also providing pressure to modernize traditional conservative values. Pope Francis recently stirred the debate among American evangelicals by issuing an encyclical on climate change that not only affirms the reality of human-caused global warming, but also issues a moral call for changes in lifestyle, consumption, and policy. This divide in the conservative theological world puts many lawmakers in a tight spot, as many have linked their faith to their political views.

"I think it's easy for Republicans to dismiss Greenpeace and other people who they see as tree-hugging leftists," said John Gehring, the Catholic program director of Faith in Public Life, a religious advocacy group in Washington, DC. "It's much harder for them to brush off one of the greatest moral leaders of the world."

THE CHANGING FACE OF PROGRESSIVE MOVEMENTS

The policy carcasses lie also at the other end of the traditional spectrum. Unlike the conservatives, progressives blame corporate agenda and influence for inequality, high poverty rates, and environmental problems. They argue for more laws, regulation, and intervention on the part of governments. They don't mind bigger governments and higher taxes. They say social programs are needed to help the victims of the market economy, which they tend to view with suspicion – though of course we all participate in it every day. Too often their solutions are simply calls for more government spending. The shopping lists are long.

Underlying it all is the notion that we should be responsible for one another. That basic tenet is why I am more at home on that end of the spectrum. But solutions that improve social and environmental conditions are much different than I once thought. Is an increase to social assistance going to help families in Garden Hill First Nation? Is more healthcare spending going to address our problem with increased incidence of diet-related disease? Will more spending on urban sprawl address our infrastructure deficits? None of these problems require bigger government.

A NEW PARADIGM

For both conservatives and progressives, the social enterprise model stretches the bounds of conventional thinking while also appealing to underlying values. The new dimension for progressives is being open to market mechanisms and expressing a desire to make government smaller. I see more and more progressives making this shift, though for the most part the people pushing the solutions sector are not involved in party politics.

In past years much of the energy and creativity in the NDP has come from rank and file union members, anti-poverty activists, farmers, and others. Now I see progressive energy and creativity in the small farm movement, the green-energy sector, and social enterprises. But these folks, for the most part, are not to be found at an NDP convention. For the problem-solving sector, governmental politics is most often seen as an obstacle rather than a vehicle for change. Political parties are perceived as too constraining, too stuck in defending old paradigms.

The beginnings of a radical shift are taking place within our familiar political spectrum, and these changes have everything to do with the solutions economy. Parties that continue to defend our existing food system and advocate for increasing incarceration rates, urban sprawl, and fossil fuels will become less and less relevant. Conservatives will need to be a lot less supportive of big corporations. Progressives will have to be more entrepreneurial and differentiate between good and bad government to capture the hearts of activists. Relevant political parties will need to be a lot more solutions-oriented.

In the new paradigm, imagine the small farm movement and its alliance with conservatives who hunt, fish, and conserve land? And anti-poverty activists joining the Chambers of Commerce as social entrepreneurs who run non-profit businesses that hire people with no access to the labour market. And green progressives who want government rules to promote mass adoption of small-scale energy solutions, rather than large, government-owned energy projects.

AGREE TO AGREE?

If political parties appeal to peoples' values, rather than their ideologies, conservatives and progressives should be able to agree on the Basic Income Guarantee, a higher minimum wage, and social enterprises. They should work together on these things. Political parties have their own cultures and traditional approaches to problems. Conservatives, like progressives, see their world view as common sense. Anything outside it is just plain wrong. But we all need to be nimble in our thinking. We need to be open to new possibilities, especially when those new possibilities are consistent with our core beliefs. We need not be afraid of solutions. And we need to be open to the possibility that the best solutions may not be the ones we have been advocating for but ones that combine values from both sides in creative new ways.

The new paradigm is about small-scale economic ventures that are solving social and environmental problems. The solutions economy is both entrepreneurial and compassionate. It is both market-based and focused on good social outcomes. Political parties need to recognize and support these policy spaces and program structures for this new approach to flourish and realize its vast potential.

Solutions transcend the old boundaries. Solutions bring people together rather than drawing dividing lines.

GOLDEN BOY

In 2011, I was standing in a crowd of about 500 people in front of the Manitoba Legislature during a rally to oppose the tough-on-crime agenda. We were all angry and disappointed. Angry that governments were pretending to be tough on crime instead of promoting employment solutions and disappointed that our provincial government would support such an inhumane and expensive agenda.

I heard my name being yelled from up above. Could it be, I wondered, the Justice Minister leaning out a window to say that the government was going to focus more resources on crime prevention? It took me a moment to identify the source of the voice. Then I saw Bruce Carson. He was beaming with pride up on the roof of the Legislature. He had a hard hat on his head, a tool belt around his waist, and a confident smile on his face. He was part of a work crew making improvements to the Manitoba Legislative Building.

When I first met Bruce Carson, he didn't need a longer sentence, he didn't need more police to track him down, and he didn't need to be sitting idle in a prison cell. He needed a place to drop off a resume and a path to employment.

CONCLUSION
AN ARMY OF PROBLEM SOLVERS

It was 7 a.m. on October 31, 2015. I was spending Halloween in North-lands Denesuline First Nation, a tight-knit community of 800 people in Northern Manitoba, 80 kilometres from the Nunavut border. The sun wouldn't be up for a while that far north, but it was a good morning for a walk. Northlands lies on the shore of beautiful Lac Brochet. The October snow was falling as I walked, covering up the ice-skating marks left on the lake from a rigorous hockey game the night before. The only sound was a couple of dogs barking in the distance. Other than that it was dark and dead still.

There is no year-round road access to Northlands. Everything is flown in at great cost unless it comes in on the winter road, which is open for six weeks in late winter. The Dene are remarkably resilient despite more than a century of unfulfilled treaty obligations. By some estimates the Dene have been in the North for 3,000 years. While they are in no way related to the Cree, Ojibway, or Dakota, some of their ancestors migrated south-ward about 1,000 years ago and became the Navajo in Arizona.

While in Northlands I learned that the caribou would be coming soon. They were near Tadoule Lake, just a few hundred kilometres away. And when they come, they come. Sometimes in the thousands. The community practically empties out. Soon there will be meat to be shared around.

But trouble lies beneath all the beauty in the remote community. It comes in the form of high unemployment, high poverty rates, and high diabetes, among other things. Like all low-income communities, there is basically no local economy. There is the Northern Store and a woman selling bannock tacos out of her house. You can order stuff online and get it flown in, but that's about it.

In addition to what other First Nations have to deal with, North-lands isn't connected to the provincial electricity grid. That means diesel fuel is hauled in on the winter roads to be used in furnaces and to generate electricity. The diesel used for space heating is stored in tanks beside the buildings with pipes leading to the buildings. The tanks are prone to leak, or they are overfilled causing spillage, or the fuel leaks, undetected, between the tank and the heating furnace inside. Most of the community is, in effect, a contaminated site. There are wet spots in the soil everywhere. Kids breath in the fumes. Everyone does.

There is more money spent on diesel and its cleanup than on housing, economic development, and healthy food combined. It is another instance of abundant government money available to spend on a problem. The diesel is job killing, brutally expensive, unhealthy, and environmentally backward.

On my flight into Northlands from Winnipeg, I met reps from a soil-remediation company who were familiar with the community. They had been there many times before on lucrative government contracts. They were on their way to undertake a half-million-dollar contract to take soil samples and come up with a remediation plan. A multi-million-dollar contract to actually clean up the soil would follow. None of this creates any local jobs.

Big business won't solve the problems, and evidently big government won't either. Oil companies, trucking companies, and soil remediation companies make millions while the Dene are left with fumes and the taxpayers are left with a huge bill.

Manitoba Hydro has a legislated monopoly on electricity sales in Manitoba, which makes it against the law for the Dene to set up their own renewable power company to generate and sell electricity.

Of course, it doesn't have to be this way.

AMPLE OPPORTUNITY

Diesel fuel isn't the only thing leaking at Northlands. Nearly all the money spent on food, energy, goods, and services leaks out of the community. That is both the problem and the opportunity. What is needed is a problem solver and the tools to redirect the money spent on problems toward solutions.

At a community meeting on the night before my peaceful morning walk, those gathered decided to start a social enterprise. Joe Hyslop, a former chief of Northlands and respected elder, translated what my co-worker and I had to say into Dene. Elder Hyslop told me later that he added some things into his translated version of our presentation. He added that the social enterprise model we talked about is how they used to do things. "We collected wood, we got our own food, we worked hard and looked after each other," he told the people.

They decided to call the social enterprise Konnn, which, as I understand it, is the Dene word to explain what happens in the moment the lightning strikes the ground. So Konnn Incorporated it is. The basic purpose of Konnn is to replace diesel fuel with better options. Those will include geothermal heating and burning wood (biomass) for heat.

The school is one of the most contaminated sites. Converting it to biomass would provide at least $100,000 a year in employment for community members. Konnn would pay people to collect wood and chip it rather than paying for the diesel-fuel racket. It would be cheaper than diesel, and the money would go into the community rather than to large southern companies. The work would involve harvesting wood from forest fire burn areas. Experts say that 10 percent of the wood from burns within 20 kilometres of the community could heat Northlands for 200 years.

The geothermal project would involve putting the loops in the lake to service a cluster of buildings near the shore.

The idea is to set up a utility that would sell renewable heat and renewable power to customers – mostly the federal government. The big questions to the government are two-fold: will you agree to pay for energy what you were going to pay anyway and will you work in relationship with us, cooperatively with us, to make that happen? This, as Grand Chief Sheila North Wilson says in the preface to this book, is what "Nation-to-Nation" looks like.

CONNECTING PROBLEMS AND PROBLEM SOLVERS

What has prevented change from coming sooner? Turns out it isn't the locals. It almost never is. They have been ready for some time. Hyslop tells me that when he was chief, over a decade ago, a delegation went to Quebec to see the biomass operation at Ouje-Bougoumou which I spoke about earlier.

In Konnn, Northlands has an official problem solver. But it's just an idea until colonial barriers are removed. Biomass and geothermal options would be both practical and economically viable if the federal government would agree to pay the social enterprise to provide the heat rather than paying the diesel lords. They would also need to agree to pay what they've been paying and expect to pay in the future. This would launch a biomass collection industry and expertise would be developed that would be exportable to other First Nations. This is, after all, how the economic development process works.

Though these projects stand to create employment, reduce environmental impacts – both local contamination and greenhouse gas emissions – and save Ottawa money, the federal bureaucracy is a major obstacle. Partway through a meeting about this project with senior Indigenous Affairs officials, a 28-year veteran of the department, told me that this was the best idea he'd ever seen come across his desk. The maze of rules and regulations is such that they cannot just say, "Great, give us a solid proposal and we'll work with you." *The bureaucracy is not allowed to buy renewable, job-creating heat from a social enterprise.* It doesn't work that way. They fund projects – not transformation. Transformation leads to loss of control and colonial systems depend on control.

I explain that, over time, all 170 Canadian "diesel" communities could be converted to renewable options through financing. The upfront capital costs could be paid back out of the utility bill reductions. No funding is needed. Just think "Nation-to-Nation." Set the conditions for prosperity, and it will undoubtedly emerge. But the old way still rules. The systemic commitment to the problem is both mind-boggling and tragic.

What about a farm in Northlands to raise vegetables and chickens? Tomatoes and cucumbers would do well in a greenhouse in the summertime with the long daylight hours. For this to happen, the federal healthy-food subsidy program must be revamped to ensure local food is eligible and non-profits selling exclusively healthy food are engaged. After this would surely come solar panels, wind turbines, a coffee shop, a laundromat, a recycling business, a healthy-food restaurant, and public health initiatives paid for out of the savings they will generate.

I am very hopeful about the future of Northlands. Ottawa will catch on eventually. After all, it's 2016.

THE COMING AGE OF THE PROBLEM SOLVERS

We need to switch our thinking from fighting poverty to creating prosperity. We need to shift from treating the symptoms of poverty to overcoming the obstacles along the path to prosperity. We need to move away from programs that do things for people to solutions that empower people to do things for themselves. We need to think not in terms of helping poor people cope, but in terms of creating an environment in which they can realize their productive capacity. We need to make reconciliation extend in very practical ways to as many people as possible. And we need to redefine prosperity to something broader, deeper, and more inclusive than simply economic growth.

When it floods in southern Manitoba – as it did in big ways along the Red River in 1997 and the Assiniboine River in 2014 – we call in the army for help. Joined by civilian volunteers, these soldiers rescue stranded homeowners, they assemble miles and miles of sandbag barriers, and they provide humanitarian assistance. They are fanned out all over the flood zone working with zeal and getting a lot done in a short time.

This is how I imagine the solutions economy: social enterprises, social entrepreneurs, mission focused co-ops, and the small farm movement – an army of problem solvers – plugging leaks, using common sense, taking responsibility for the greater good, and showing resourcefulness and confidence. When it comes to poverty and climate change, we need an army of problem solvers and we need it now.

These troops will emerge when governments redefine their roles to create conditions under which problem solvers can thrive. Every member of this army will save governments money and contribute to genuine societal progress. And they don't need to be called in from elsewhere. They are around us. They are with us. They are us.

Back in Northlands, I finish my morning walk. The sun is rising. It's going to be a good day.

PROBLEM
SOLVER
PROFILES

NAME OF COMPANY: IMPACT CONSTRUCTION (NON-PROFIT)

ORGANIZATION: Choices for Youth

HEADQUARTERS: St. John's, Newfoundland

ANNUAL REVENUES: $439,000.00 in 15/16

NUMBER OF EMPLOYEES: 19

FOUNDED: 2015

ACCOMPLISHMENTS:
Showcased in the Employment for Youth Toolkit as a best practice model; Nominee for the 2016/2017 World Habitat Award as part of the Building and Social Housing Foundation in Europe.

THE PROBLEM:
St John's has youth unemployment problem, and the unfortunate statistic of 10% more than the national average when it comes to youth (ages 16-29) using emergency shelters.

THE SOLUTION:
Impact Construction has evolved into a high-producing, high-outcome social enterprise. The program side, supported by Choices for Youth, provides housing support, education, legal support services, and direct connection to mental health and addiction workers. The social enterprise side provides on-the-job training and employment.

WHAT IS NEEDED TO SUPERSIZE?
More public and private contracts that provide consistent work.

WWW.IMPACTCONSTRUCTIONNL.COM

PROBLEM SOLVER PROFILE:

BUILD INC.

NAME OF COMPANY: BUILD INC. (NON-PROFIT)

HEADQUARTERS: Winnipeg's North End

ANNUAL REVENUES: $1.5 million

NUMBER OF EMPLOYEES: 45

FOUNDED: 2006

ACCOMPLISHMENTS:
Winner of EcoLiving Award for Canada's Green Business of the Year (Scotia Bank 2011), Winner Manitoba Employer of the Year (Manitoba Apprenticeship 2013), Winner Spirit Award (Winnipeg Chamber of Commerce 2016).

THE PROBLEM:
Inner-city unemployment and high utility bills in low income housing.

THE SOLUTION:
Lowered energy and/or water bills at 12,500 homes – utility bill reductions of $4 million per year. Trained 500 people.

WHAT IS NEEDED TO SUPERSIZE?
• A modern mandate for Manitoba Hydro (requirements to work with social enterprises to insulate a 2,500 homes per year for 10 years).
• Provincial legislation requiring all landlords to meet minimum efficiency standards.
• More training dollars.

WWW.BUILDINC.CA

MEECHIM INC

NAME OF COMPANY: MEECHIM INC - (NON-PROFIT, LOCAL FOOD MOVEMENT)

HEADQUARTERS: Garden Hill First Nation

ANNUAL REVENUES: $500,000

NUMBER OF EMPLOYEES: 18

FOUNDED: 2015 (non-profit) and Administered by Aki Energy

STRATEGY:
Offers bi-monthly pop-up healthy food market, healthy options at the arena, 13 acre farm with chicken barn and orchard, and school to farm initiative.

THE PROBLEM:
Rampant Diabetes, Massive Unemployment.

WHAT IS NEEDED:
Federal Government's generous support, the re-emergence of the local food economy, rejection of preferential treatment for monopoly retailer that sells mostly unhealthy food, and support for building entrepreneurship capacity.

SEE THEIR MOVIE TRAILER!
HTTPS://YOUTU.BE/FFTVVURA2JG

WWW.AKIENERGY.COM

FRESH ROOTS FARM

NAME OF COMPANY: FRESH ROOTS FARM - (LOCAL FOOD MOVEMENT)

OWNED AND OPERATED BY: Troy Stozek and Michelle Schram

HEADQUARTERS: Cartwright, MB

ANNUAL REVENUES: $150,000

THE PROBLEM:
Food related illness, rural depopulation, phosphorus-laden waters, and climate change caused by fossil fuel usage.

THE SOLUTION:
Fresh Roots uses no synthetic fertilizers and sells whole foods directly to local families. They build community by knowing their customers. They bring their 45 cows and 25 sheep to their feed (grass) rather than import feed. They have 125 bee hives as well. Soil building, rather than soil depletion, is very important at Fresh Roots. Plans are shortly to launch an online ordering system and monthly delivery to Winnipeg and surrounding area.

WHAT IS NEEDED TO SUPERSIZE?
More government purchasing of local, sustainable food would give farms like Fresh Roots a real boost and help normalize local food purchasing. Move government Department of Agriculture away from promotion of soil depleting practices to suite of policies and incentives to promote soil building. Help new farmers buy land and get started. Michelle says: "With the right mix of policies and incentives, we could bring a lot more farmers onboard."

WWW.FRESHROOTSFARMMB.COM

PROBLEM SOLVER PROFILE:
MANITOBA GREEN RETROFIT

NAME OF COMPANY: MANITOBA GREEN RETROFIT (MGR) - (NON-PROFIT)
HEADQUARTERS: WINNIPEG'S NORTH END
ANNUAL REVENUES: 1.8 MILLION
NUMBER OF EMPLOYEES: 45
FOUNDED: 2009

ACCOMPLISHMENTS:
Business Alliance for Local Living Economies (BALLE) Fellowship
(Lucas Stewart – first in Western Canada).

THE PROBLEM:
In Winnipeg, there is a large group of people who face barriers to the formal labour market.

THE SOLUTION:
85 percent of MGR's staff have barriers to employment. Work builds confidence
and self-worth which are the foundations for improving lives - meeting
people where they are at in a way that encourages success!

MGR's chosen services are crew based and labour intensive, which combine experienced supervision
with entry level positions. They focus on apartment renovations in public and non-profit housing,
bed bug remediation and demolition jobs – work that is relatively repetitive and non-seasonal.

WHAT IS NEEDED TO SUPERSIZE?
Manitoba Housing has been their most important customer. They are ready to take on more work
from them and other departments as well such as Government Services. Aided by their biggest
fans at the Winnipeg Police Service, they hope to add the City of Winnipeg to their clientele.
The government of Canada is increasing the amount of money invested in public and non-profit
housing. These dollars can be made conditional on a percentage going to social enterprises.

WWW.MGRINC.COM

BEEP

NAME OF COMPANY: BEEP (BRANDON ENERGY EFFICIENCY PROGRAM)

HEADQUARTERS: Brandon, MB

ANNUAL REVENUES: 1.7 MILLION

NUMBER OF EMPLOYEES: 26

FOUNDED: 2009

Brandon Energy Efficiency Program

ACCOMPLISHMENTS:
Trained 140 people. Built 4 single family affordable homes for low income first time homeowners and a 5-unit affordable housing rental complex. Completed exterior energy refreshes on 40 affordable housing rental units and 8 interior/exterior renovations. Lowered energy bills for 80 private affordable housing homeowners as well as lowered energy and water bills for 500 affordable housing rental units.

THE PROBLEM:
Chronic unemployment for people with barriers to employment and lack of affordable housing.

THE SOLUTION:
Address energy and water efficiency while building and renovating affordable housing all while training previously unemployed individuals with barriers to employment preparing them for employment in the private sector.

WHAT IS NEEDED TO SUPERSIZE?
More training dollars to expand program. More public partners. More land to build more affordable housing. More driver's training.

WWW.BNRC.CA

AKI ENERGY

NAME OF COMPANY: AKI ENERGY - (NON-PROFIT)
HEADQUARTERS: FISHER RIVER CREE NATION
ANNUAL REVENUES: 2.5 MILLION
NUMBER OF EMPLOYEES: 25
FOUNDED: 2013

ACCOMPLISHMENTS:
Installed $6 million geothermal on First Nations and mentored 2
new First Nation social enterprises. Trained 50 people.

THE PROBLEM:
First Nation unemployment and economic leakage.

WHAT IS WORKING:
Partnerships with Manitoba Hydro.

THE SOLUTION:
Policy environment to allow First Nations across Canada to generate
and sell renewable energy - a "utility" approach.

WHAT IS NEEDED TO SUPERSIZE?
A partnership with Indigenous and Northern Affairs Canada and
the Canadian Mortgage and Housing Corporation.

WWW.AKIENERGY.COM

FISHER RIVER CREE BUILDERS

NAME OF COMPANY: FISHER RIVER CREE BUILDERS - (NON-PROFIT)

HEADQUARTERS: FISHER RIVER CREE NATION (MANITOBA)

REVENUES: $4 MILLION (SINCE 2013)

NUMBER OF EMPLOYEES: 12

ACCOMPLISHMENTS:
Geothermal retrofits on 200 homes and 3 commercial installs
(a carwash, fitness centre, and health centre).

THE PROBLEM:
Lack of employment opportunities and high energy bills.

WHAT IS WORKING:
Partnerships with Manitoba Hydro.

WHAT IS NEEDED TO SUPERSIZE?
Partnership with Indigenous and Northern Affairs Canada and
Pay-As-You-Save across Canada's First Nations

WWW.FISHERRIVER.COM

DIVERSITY FOOD SERVICES

NAME OF COMPANY: DIVERSITY FOOD SERVICES - (NON-PROFIT)

HEADQUARTERS: Winnipeg

ANNUAL REVENUES: $2.9 MILLION

NUMBER OF EMPLOYEES: 84

FOUNDED: 2009

DIVERSITY food services

ACCOMPLISHMENTS:
Hiring inner city students. More than half of the food sourced from local food movement. Providing all food services at University of Winnipeg.

THE PROBLEM:
Lack of jobs for inner city residents in respectful and culturally supportive workplaces, need for healthy food choices in food establishments (particularly for students), food not being sourced locally or ethically, lack of ecological business practices.

WHAT'S WORKING:
Progressive procurement at University of Winnipeg.

THE SOLUTION:
More progressive procurement at public and private institutions.

WHAT IS NEEDED TO SUPERSIZE?
Easier access to equity and patient loans
More training dollars
Greater awareness of impact of social enterprise

BUILDING UP - TORONTO

NAME OF COMPANY: BUILDING UP
HEADQUARTERS: Toronto
NUMBER OF EMPLOYEES: 20
INCORPORATED: 2014

THE PROBLEM:
Connecting multiple-barriered people in Toronto with employment.
Nearly 200 people recently applied for 8 training positions.

PROGRESS TO DATE:
5,000 water retrofits and 400 million litres annual reduction in water usage

WHAT IS CONNECTING PROBLEM TO PROBLEM SOLVER?
Michael Bloomberg awarded Building Up with $100,000 in start-up
money for emerging social entrepreneurs.

WHAT IS NEEDED TO GROW?
Progressive, modern procurement in public
and non-profit housing in Toronto and the GTA.

WWW.BUIDLINGUP.CA